TOM JONES

TOM JONES

A Film Script

by

John Osborne

Film Book Editor: Robert Hughes

GROVE PRESS, INC.   NEW YORK

CAST

Squire Allworthy's House

SQUIRE ALLWORTHY	George Devine
BRIDGET ALLWORTHY	Rachel Kempson
MRS. WILKINS	Angela Baddeley
JENNY JONES (MRS. WATERS)	Joyce Redman
PARTRIDGE	Jack MacGowran
TOM JONES	Albert Finney
MOLLY SEAGRIM	Diane Cilento
BLACK GEORGE	Wilfrid Lawson
SQUARE	John Moffatt
THWACKUM	Peter Bull
BLIFIL	David Warner
MRS. SEAGRIM	Freda Jackson
LAWYER DOWLING	Redmond Phillips

Squire Western's House

SQUIRE WESTERN	Hugh Griffith
SOPHIE WESTERN	Susannah York
PARSON SUPPLE	James Cairncross
MISS WESTERN	Edith Evans
HONOR	Patsy Rowlands

On the Road to London

LIEUTENANT	Mark Dignam
NORTHERTON	Julian Glover
LANDLADY, GEORGE INN	Avis Bunnage
MRS. FITZPATRICK	Rosalind Knight
SUSAN, UPTON INN	Lynn Redgrave
MR. FITZPATRICK	George A. Cooper
MAC LACHLAN	Jack Stewart

London

LADY BELLASTON	Joan Greenwood
MRS. MILLER	Rosalind Atkinson
LORD FELLAMAR	David Tomlinson

Narration spoken by Micháel MacLiammóir

PRODUCTION CREDITS

Screenplay by John Osborne
Based on the novel by Henry Fielding
Music composed and conducted by John Addison
Played by Sinfonia of London

Production Designer	Ralph Brinton
Color Consultant	Jocelyn Herbert
Art Director	Ted Marshall
Director of Photography	Walter Lassally
Film Editor	Antony Gibbs
Camera Operator	Desmond Davis
Sound Recordist	Peter Handford
Assistant Editor	Brian Smedley-Aston
Second Unit Photographer	Manny Wynn
Sound Editor	Don Challis
Set Decorator	Josie Mac Avin
Assistant to Miss Herbert	Clare Jefferey
Chief Make-up	Alex Garfath
Chief Hairdresser	Sarah Beeber
Wardrobe Supervisor	John McCorry
Wardrobe Mistress	Barbara Gillett
Continuity	Rita Davison
Production Secretary	Jane Moscrop
Personal Assistant to the Director	Jocelyn Tawse
Assistant Director	Gerry O'Hara
Script Editor	Sewell Stokes
Production Executive	Alan Kaplan
Production Supervisor	Leigh Aman
Production Manager	Ray Millichip
Associate Producers	Michael Holden, Oscar Lewenstein

Produced and Directed by Tony Richardson

*The première was held on June 26, 1963
at the London Pavilion*

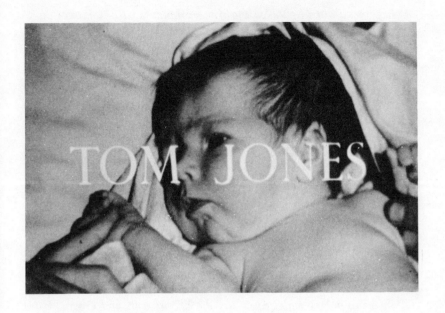

TOM JONES

EXTERIOR. ALLWORTHY'S HOUSE. DUSK.

TITLE: In the West of England there was once a Squire Allworthy. After several months in London he returns home.

A long avenue of beech trees stretches toward a distant road seen through the arch of the gatehouse. A coach drawn by four horses comes up to camera and, as it arrives, the camera reveals the Allworthy house, a sixteenth-century mansion.

TITLE: His Sister Bridget.

The main door of the house is opened and servants excitedly pour out. Camera pans Miss Bridget Allworthy as she greets her brother Squire Allworthy, a simple, kindly middle-aged wid-

ower, with an affectionate kiss as he steps out of the coach.

TITLE: His Servants.

They move out of shot as the camera holds on the servants unloading the luggage supervised by Squire Allworthy's housekeeper, Mrs. Wilkins.

TITLE: After supper.

INTERIOR. ALLWORTHY'S HOUSE. HALL/STUDY. NIGHT.

We are looking into the Allworthy hall where dinner has just taken place. The house is glowing with the lick of swaying candlelight, the laughter of Mr. Allworthy and his sister as they finish their dinner, and the pleasure of the servants in having their master home. Allworthy and Miss Allworthy rise and come toward camera. They kiss good night and camera pans Allworthy up the stairs.

ALLWORTHY'S BEDROOM.

Allworthy enters and begins to take off his coat and cravat. He goes behind a screen, emerges in his nightshirt, and comes toward the large four-poster. Camera tracks with Allworthy until the four-poster bed is revealed in the foreground. He kneels to say his prayers, when his eyes are riveted to an object in his bed. He recoils and turns.

TITLE: "Mrs. Wilkins."

STAIRCASE.

Camera pans Mrs. Wilkins thundering upstairs like a routed goose from below.

BEDROOM.

Allworthy leans over to lift the bedcovers.
Mrs. Wilkins opens the door to Allworthy's bedroom only to reveal the full length of her master clad only in his nightshirt.

8

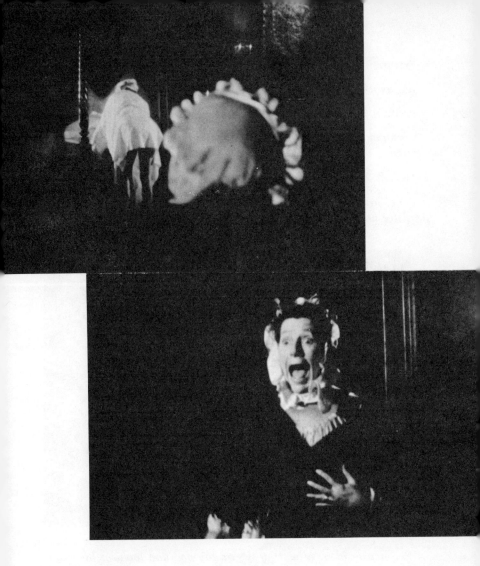

She screams.

TITLE: "Aaah!"

Allworthy rushes to the door and brings her in. They go to the four-poster; Allworthy looks at her demandingly and points to the object. The camera zooms in on a small baby lying fast asleep on the bed.

TITLE: "A baby."

TITLE: "Abandoned."

Allworthy inquires.

TITLE: "How did it get here?"

Bridget Allworthy enters and the camera pans with her to the bed.

TITLE: "Who can the mother be?"

The Squire shakes his head and raises his hands in despair. His sister notes his obvious bafflement. Mrs. Wilkins look on beadily.

She has an idea. Allworthy sits on the bed and looks at his sister, who averts her eyes and looks down at the baby. We pan on to the baby who opens its eyes and gurgles. Mrs. Wilkins leaves.

TITLE: "Jenny Jones."

STAIRS.

Mrs. Wilkins pulls a frightened Jenny upstairs. She is dressed in a shift. Camera pans with them.

10

BEDROOM.

The door opens as Jenny is propelled forward by Mrs. Wilkins.
Allworthy is now standing. Jenny Jones is a large, rosy, not
too comely, but intelligent girl. Bridget looks very distressed.
But Allworthy is doing his magistrate's best at the moment, and
looking very stern.

TITLE: "Who is the father, Jenny?"

Jenny, kneeling in close shot, shakes her head.

TITLE: "Sir, I am under the most solemn ties not to reveal the
father's name."

Mrs. Wilkins turns toward the landing.

TITLE: "Send for Partridge the barber!"

Partridge is bustled into the room by two servants.

TITLE: "Partridge the barber—the father?"

Allworthy gives him a look.

TITLE: "I will deal with you later, sir."

11

Allworthy turns on Jenny. Jenny cringes.

TITLE: "You must be sent away from this shame and degradation."

The Squire sighs.

TITLE: "As to your child . . ."

Bridget on the bed by the baby. Jenny still on her knees.

TITLE: "I will bring him up as if he were my own son."

Jenny bursts into tears of gratitude. Bridget with the baby. Mrs. Wilkins and the servants and Jenny move to leave. Allworthy sits on the bed with the baby between him and his sister. We begin to track in on the baby.

TITLE: "What will you call him, brother?"

Allworthy considers.

TITLE: "Tom Jones."

TITLE: "Of whom the opinion of all was that he was born to be hanged."

The credits follow, superimposed still on the close-up of the baby. He plays with the fingers of Bridget and Allworthy. As the last credit fades out we flip to:

WOODS. NIGHT.

Tom is moving through the moonlit trees. Camera tracks before him. He is now twenty years old.

COMMENTATOR: Our hero grew apace. . . .

A crisp April night in the deep woods. Camera looking up through trees, pans to clouds, crossing a moon whose light blinks through the trees. Pan continues until it ends in a close shot of Tom by a tree, listening and watching. His breath rises like a tiny mist in the cold night as:

COMMENTATOR: A country lad, far happier in the woods than in the study. As bad a hero as may be, with many a weakness, but then—

Tom's eyeline: A fox scuds through the trees. A beaver runs past.

Close-up: Tom, moving with his gun. Tom's eyeline: An owl winks. Owl's eyeline: Tom winks back.

COMMENTATOR: If Adam hadn't had such a weakness for apples there would be nobody to tell Tom's story at all, and a part of that story tells of the sport Tom found in the woods.

13

WOODS. BY SEAGRIM'S COTTAGE.

Suddenly from beside a tree Molly rises.

MOLLY: Oh Tom, you wicked dog!

TOM: Molly . . . What are you doing here?

MOLLY: I heard father tell mother you was coming. (*She looks at him, flipping a fern.*)

He trips on his way to her. She laughs. They are together beside the tree.

TOM: It's a good night to be abroad and looking for game.

He puts his arms around her, which she's obviously used to.

MOLLY: Oh, Tom! Oh, Tom!

They sink, laughing together, onto the soft mossy bank beneath the trees. Their games continue behind a bush.

COMMENTATOR: It shall be our custom to relieve such scenes where taste and decorum and the censor dictate. . . . In this way we shall try to make up for our incorrigible hero.

WOODS. NEAR DAWN.

Two dark figures slipping through the trees. Black George, the gamekeeper, with a dog and gun, stalking the woods with Tom.

COMMENTATOR: As soon as he had left the disreputable Molly, what did he do but join her equally disreputable father, Black George, gamekeeper to Squire Allworthy.

TOM: There's little about tonight.

They slip off quietly through the woods. We pan with them.

EDGE OF WOODS.

A slight mist rises at the edge of the woods. The figures of Tom and the gamekeeper emerge out of the wood. Suddenly they start. Eyeline: A covey of pheasant rise.
Tom raises his shotgun and fires. He exchanges it with Black George and fires again. Eyeline: A pheasant falls.

TOM: Come on.

WESTERN'S SPINNEY.

On Squire Western's estate, Squire Western peering into the night breathing heavily and snorting. He is accompanied by three or four retainers with guns silhouetted against a more broken bit of wood.

EDGE OF WOODS.

The partridges rise again in foreground of shot. In the background Tom and Black George fire.

16

WESTERN'S SPINNEY.

Squire Western sniffs the air like a slightly drunken dog and growls at his servants crouched beside him.

WESTERN: I hear 'em, I hear 'em. Come on, lads, we'll smoke 'em out! Fetch it, fetch it, boy.

They all move forward with a whoop of noise.

WOODS.

TOM: Come on.

The dog runs for the bird.

BLACK GEORGE: Wait, that's fallen on Squire Western's land.

TOM: Well, let's after it.

BLACK GEORGE: No. I've been warned for trespassing.

TOM: It's our bird. Don't worry, Blackie.

Excitedly he rushes on. Reluctantly Black George follows into the scrub. We pan with him.

Running shot: Tom has got a bird. Western's guns firing.

BLACK GEORGE: Come back. Come . . .

TOM: Here boy, here boy, here boy . . .

OPEN FIELD.

Western and his men break into the open ground and then wheel back into the field. Squire Western dances in the moonlight.

WESTERN: All right, you devils, I'll get you . . . (*Gunfire.*) I'll have your blood. I'll—(*Gunfire.*)

EDGE OF WOODS.

More gunfire. Tom roaring with laughter joins Black George in the woods. Tom rushes through the trees, the dog yelping behind.

TOM: Run, Blackie. Let's give the old lad a run for his money.

Camera pans him into the darkness of thick undergrowth.

OPEN FIELD.

Squire Western snorts off.

WESTERN: Home, lads. I'll get them another night.

SEAGRIM'S COTTAGE. BACKYARD.

Tom arrives out of breath and laughing. Black George more fearful.

TOM: I thought I lost you in the woods.

BLACK GEORGE: Short cut. We'll get caught one of these days.

TOM: Don't worry.

BLACK GEORGE: It's all right for you, you haven't got a family to keep.

TOM: I'll look after you. Here, take this guinea. Goodnight, Blackie.

Tom gives Black George the coin and turns to go. Camera holds

18

on Black George as he pockets the money and looks contemptuously after Tom.

COMMENTATOR: Our hero, alas, was always being exploited by villains like Black George. For a generous man is merely a fool in the eyes of a thief.

Black George turns to the outhouse door and discovers the constable standing in wait for him beckoning. Black George becomes acutely aware of the large sheep's carcass hanging on the back of the door directly between himself and the constable. The constable is pointing at the sheep's head as the camera zooms in on it. Two speeches from the next scene are heard here.

ALLWORTHY: A sheep. . . .

THWACKUM: Aye, sir, an entire sheep.

INTERIOR: ALLWORTHY'S STUDY. DAY.

The hearing is in process.

SQUARE: A fat animal, enough to feed a village for a week.

BLIFIL: Hanging up in his cottage as proud as a battle trophy.

ALLWORTHY: This is a grave matter.

THWACKUM: A hanging matter!

TOM: Sir, if I may speak on his behalf, I'd like—

ALLWORTHY: Silence! Are you guilty?

Black George rolls his eyes dully at his accusers.

BLACK GEORGE: I—am—gu—guilty.

TOM: Sir, forgive him—

ALLWORTHY: Be quiet, sir. I have to give justice here.

Tom is furious with the accusers.

ALLWORTHY (*continues to Black George*): You have committed a capital crime. The laws have provided the most terrible penalty—to hang by the neck.

Black George seems about to shake. Allworthy studies him and faces the others for a few moments.

ALLWORTHY: But you have children. For their sake I shall only dismiss you from my service. And may God have mercy on you.

Black George rolls his eyes like a baffled dog, and then shuffles out with the constable. Thwackum and Square stand looking cheated.

THWACKUM: You're too lenient, Mr. Allworthy—

SQUARE: Compassion is one thing, sir, but Justice is another.

The image of the four is frozen.

COMMENTATOR: Mr. Thwackum and Mr. Square were Tom's tutors. . . .

EXTERIOR. ALLWORTHY'S HOUSE. DAY.

Tom is lying on the terrace cleaning his gun. The camera zooms back.

COMMENTATOR: Over the years they tried with little success to thrash into Tom a sense of virtue and religion. They had, however, a more apt pupil.

ALLWORTHY'S FORMAL GARDEN.

Allworthy is inspecting the espalier trees with one of his gardeners. Camera still moving has now panned to where Bridget is gathering an armful of flowers.

COMMENTATOR: Soon after Tom had been found, the Squire's sister Bridget was married to Captain Blifil, and they had a son. This young man was quite different from Tom. He was sober, discreet and pious beyond his age, and the whole neighborhood resounded in his praise.

Camera continues panning and cranes up and over the yew hedges to look into the formal garden where Blifil, a tall correct youth who looks roughly the same age as Tom joins his two tutors, Thwackum and Square. They are just finishing a lesson and coming back. Tom's eyeline of Blifil and the tutors coming through the hedge. Tracking shot.

SQUARE: You have only taught Tom to laugh at whatever is decent and virtuous and right.

THWACKUM: I've taught him religion . . .

SQUARE: Well! The word religion is as vague and uncertain as any in the English language.

THWACKUM: When I mention religion I mean the Christian religion, not only the Christian religion but the Protestant religion, and not only the Protestant religion but the Church of England.

SQUARE: I fear that Tom is the embodiment of the old truth: that bastards should be left to the parish.

BLIFIL: My dear tutors. I'm afraid neither of you can touch his bastard's heart.

All three nod in agreement. Dissolve.

MOSSY BANK. WOODS BY SEAGRIM'S COTTAGE. NIGHT.

COMMENTATOR: Aye, that indeed, but there was another that could.

Two dim shapes. It is Tom and Molly lying beside each other, looking relaxed.

MOLLY: Tom—

TOM: Mmmm—

MOLLY: I want you to help me.

TOM: How?

Molly fingers his nose and mouth.

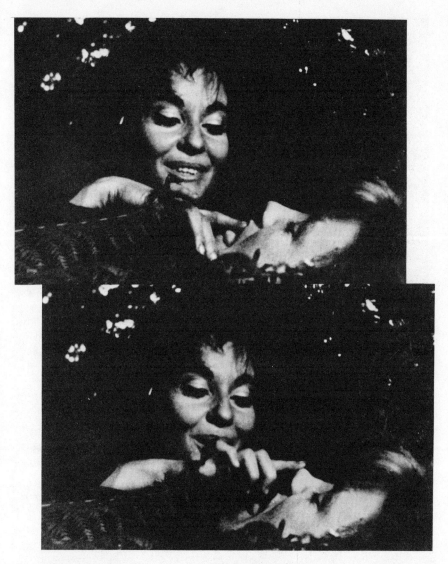

MOLLY: I want you to get me a post, Tom.

TOM: Ahhhh—

MOLLY: Miss Western's come back from France and will be wanting a maid.

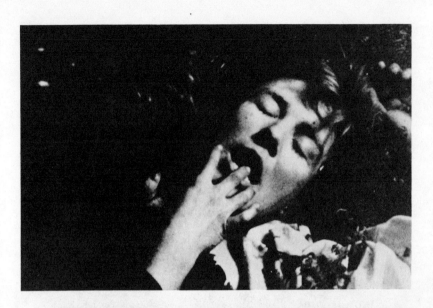

TOM: I'll speak to her.

MOLLY: You're kind to me. (*She gives him a big, wet kiss and leans back.*) Miss Western's maid . . .

BRIDGE BY LAKE. SQUIRE WESTERN'S. DAY.

Sophie, beautiful daughter of Squire Western. Swans come for bread which she throws to them, dissolving her reflection for a moment. Tom's voice is heard off. Camera tracks in front of Tom as he canters gently along singing to himself, full of the joy of life. He has a small bird in a cage.

TOM: Miss Western! Miss Western!

SOPHIE: Why, Tom Jones!

Tom and Sophie are at either side of the bridge; Tom runs to her. He gives the bird to her. She is delighted.

TOM: I've brought you a thrush.

SOPHIE: Oh, oh, it's beautiful, Tom. How kind of you.

TOM: Two years is a long time, Sophie. (*He sits with his legs spanning the bridge.*) Did they teach you London ways and make a great lady of you?

25

SOPHIE: Most of the time I was in France. My Aunt took me there.

TOM (*impressed*): Oo-la-la . . . And did you like France, Miss Western?

SOPHIE (*laughing at his awesomeness*): Mais oui, Monsieur. Je suis très amusé, merci.

TOM: Bon, bon.

SOPHIE: You haven't changed, Tom.

TOM: You've grown Sophie—grown more beautiful than ever.

The bird sings. Tom and Sophie stroll along the bridge.

SOPHIE: Doesn't he sing beautifully? I'll teach him some new songs.

TOM: I doubt if an English bird can learn French songs, Miss Western.

SOPHIE: You'll see. "Sur le pont d'Avignon . . ."

They both laugh as Sophie takes the bird out of the cage. It has a thin thread attached to its leg. Tom feeds the bird.

TOM: Your father asked us all to supper. I've come early to ask you if you could help Molly, Black George's daughter.

SOPHIE: Oh, yes. Father told me the story. He stole a sheep, didn't he?

TOM: Black George is a poor man. He's big hungry daughters to feed. (*Thinking of Molly with a bite of bird food in his mouth. Tom glances at the camera.*) Most hungry—I can vouch for it.

SOPHIE: Well, I have a maid already, Tom, but I'll see if I can do anything.

TOM: Good, good, good.

EXTERIOR. WESTERN'S HOUSE.

Camera looking toward house: Allworthy, Thwackum, Mrs. Blifil, Square and Blifil ride up. Squire Western comes out of the house to greet his guests.

WESTERN (*he shouts off*): Ah, welcome. Welcome, neighbors.

Western and the Allworthy group cross the lawn from the house. There are general greetings all around.

WESTERN: Squire—

ALLWORTHY: Good day, Western. Good day.

Sophie and Tom run toward them.

SOPHIE: Look! Tom has brought me a thrush.

She passes the cage along the line.

BRIDGET: Ah, what a sweet little bird.

SOPHIE: His song is sweeter than any tune of Mr. Handel.

WESTERN: Agh! Handel! Agh . . .

SOPHIE: Tom, thank you—

WESTERN: She'll dote on it.

Blifil has the cage. He reaches inside it.

BRIDGET: Welcome home, Sophie. How lovely you're looking, child.

WESTERN: Aye, it's good to have her home.

ALLWORTHY: Good day, Miss Western.

SOPHIE: Squire—

WESTERN: Let's all go in to dinner.

Sophie turns and Blifil, who is in the extreme foreground of frame, with an offhand and adroit gesture throws the bird into the air. We pan with it.

BLIFIL: Oh, dear.

Sophie and Tom.

SOPHIE (*crying out*): Oh my little bird!

They all watch the bird. The bird flutters a moment with the thread dangling from its leg. Finally it alights on a branch over-

hanging the lake. Tom runs to the foot of the tree.

TOM: Don't worry, Sophie. I'll get it back for you.

Quietly, expertly, Tom climbs the tree. Close shot: Sophie.

SOPHIE: Tom. . . .

WESTERN: Aye, good lad, Tom.

The group is watching Tom, with Sophie and Blifil in foreground.

SQUARE: Do be careful . . .

SOPHIE: Be careful, Tom. Tom, take care. Take care.

SQUARE: I wager he gets it.

BLIFIL: I am sorry to cause you this distress, Miss Western. I did not think the bird would fly away. But still I cannot help observing that the idea of caged birds is against the laws of nature—don't you agree, Mr. Square?

Western snorts. But Sophie is not listening. She is intent on Tom's climb. Tom is now climbing along the branch where the bird is perched. He whistles softly to it, as he edges nearer. Slowly he slides his hand on to grasp the string.

BLIFIL (*suddenly shouting and clapping his hands to alert the bird*): He's got him!

Tom makes a grab and goes tumbling down into the muddy water.

Sophie screams and rushes to the side of the lake.

SOPHIE: Oh, oh! He'll drown! Quick! Get him out, get him out! Help him, someone.

The others cluster around by the edge of the lake as Tom gets up. He is about up to his shoulders in mud and festooned with water lilies. His wig is floating on the water and he rescues it and tries to put it on.

SQUIRE WESTERN (*shouting from the bank*): Damn me if I don't love the boy for this, the longest day I have to live.

Blifil is standing on the bridge with Square and Thwackum. Blifil is smiling with satisfaction. Tom picks his way out of the water.

BLIFIL: Serves him right.

Sophie turns and hears him. In indignation she suddenly turns on him.

SOPHIE: And you, sir.

She gives him a great push into the water. All the party join in the joke except the dripping Blifil. Squire Western biffs Tom on the back and hugs him. The scene freezes.

THE SEAGRIM COTTAGE. BACKYARD. DAY.

COMMENTATOR: The weeks passed and Molly grew apace too. . . .

It is some months later. Molly is sitting disconsolately while Mrs. Seagrim and her two daughters are chopping wood and washing a few rags. Mrs. Seagrim prods Molly angrily and Molly pushes her away.

MRS. SEAGRIM: Why, you lazy slut you. Look at her, the great belly idle. Oh that I should ever see this day.

First daughter is chopping wood.

FIRST DAUGHTER: You'd better have minded what the parson said and not harkened after menfolk.

MRS. SEAGRIM (*washing away*): She is the first of this family ever to be a whore.

MOLLY: Ah, mother, you yourself was brought to bed with sister there a week after you was married!

Black George comes out of cottage and the scruffy dogs littering the yard cluster around him.

MRS. SEAGRIM (*enraged, crosses to him*): Ah, but I was made an honest woman of. But you, you have to be doing with a gentleman, you nasty slut! You know what you'll have, don't you? You'll have a bastard, and I defy anyone to say that of me!

MOLLY: My gentleman will look after me.

MRS. SEAGRIM: Your gentleman! Ah, far from gentleman . . .

She cracks Molly across the chops, who staggers back into her sisters. The women all start screaming. Black George, appalled by this furious gaggle, starts laying into them all like a demented huntsman in a kennel.

MOLLY: You lay off me, or I'll tell my gentleman—

INTERIOR. CHURCH. DAY.

Parson Supple has just commenced service. The Allworthy and Western households are conspicuous in their pews. The Squire is already asleep. Sophie awakens him and Tom smiles.

SUPPLE: . . . if these be properly applied. And then . . .

The Black George family enter late, finding seats at the back of the chancel. Glances from all directions are shot expectantly toward the sight of the pregnant Molly.

SUPPLE: . . . we cannot absolutely promise success, yet we may properly say with the Apostle, "What knowest thou a wife whether thou shalt save thy husband."

Tom winks at Molly, then realizes she is pregnant. He looks uncomfortable.

SUPPLE: And now, my dear brethren, let us sing together the hymn, "Oh God Our Help in Ages Past."

Everyone sings, Tom with great gusto: "Oh God our help in ages past, our hope for years to come . . ."

EXTERIOR. CHURCH.

Everyone is coming out, the members of the Western and All-worthy households first. Camera pans to a large group centered around Goody Brown, a flat-chested virago.

COMMENTATOR:
>Let dogs delightful bark and bite, for God has made them so,
>Let bears and lions growl and fight for 'tis their nature to,
>But ladies you should never let such angry passions rise,
>Your little hands were never made to tear each others' eyes.

Close shot: Molly at the church door. Reaction shot from the group. Molly tosses her head and camera tracks with her in close shot through the crowd. Goody Brown picks up a lump of mud and hurls it at Molly. Shouts of "There she is." "Let's get her." "Take that, you, hussy." Etc.

Camera in close-up of Molly as the mud crashes against her.

She turns, looking for a weapon. Goody Brown has cast the first stone, and Mrs. Seagrim and her other two daughters flee in terror as the dirt and rubbish start to fly, and the Somerset mob roar forth an halloo. After her first shock and distress, Molly rises up in rage against this ugly looking army, taking up a skull and then a thighbone and pitching both at them furiously. Camera pans among the tombstones as a wild and brutal fight ensues. The women, howling and screaming, tear, punch and kick at each other.

LANE OUTSIDE CHURCH.

The Western and Allworthy groups, who already are a little way down the lane, turn. Molly, in distress, about to be belted in her breasts by Goody Brown. Tom leaps from his horse, camera panning, and lays about him. Tom puts an end to the fight by taking his horsewhip to the mob. Molly tries to hold together her torn dress. Tom goes to her and they embrace.

MOLLY: Tom, Tom. Please, Tom. Don't, don't leave me, Tom.

TOM: Don't worry.

Tom kisses her. He carries her to his horse and leads her off.

34

Goody Brown spits at Molly. Thwackum looks cheated again.

THWACKUM: That filthy slut.

Reaction shot of Sophie and Western as Tom disappears.

WESTERN: Good boy, good boy . . . He's a game lad, your Tom.

Sophie looks distressed. Squire Western chortles knowingly. Laughter continues over cut to next scene.

INTERIOR. WESTERN'S HOUSE. HALL. NIGHT.

Food being shoveled into Western's face. Camera pans to close-up. The whole scene to be shot in close-up with inserts on the food, on mouths chewing, glasses being drained, creating an impression of the monstrous eating habits of the period. Parson Supple is having dinner with Sophie and her father. Old Western is screeching with laughter.

WESTERN: So the wench is having a bastard?

SUPPLE: Yes, it seems the girl has refused to name the father to Mr. Allworthy. He may have to send her to Bridewell.

Sophie is blushing and looks obviously troubled. She starts to rise and ask to be excused.

SOPHIE: Father, I have a headache.

WESTERN: I smoke it!

He slaps his horny old thighs in triumph.

WESTERN: Tom is the father of this bastard.

Sophie's face crumples more than ever as the old juggins rattles on excitedly.

WESTERN: Aye, aye, sure as twopence. Tom is the bastard's father.

SOPHIE (*faintly*): Father—

WESTERN: Ods zodikins, what a little whoremaster that boy is!

SUPPLE (*sucking on a goose bone*): The girl is ruined surely.

WESTERN: Aye, ruined, ruined, to be sure! Once broken never mended!

He nearly has a fit and chokes at his joke.

WESTERN: It will do no harm. Ask Sophie. She knows about Tom. You have no worse opinion of a young fellow for getting a bastard, have you girl?

Long shot: Sophie rises.

WESTERN: Will you, will you stop bobbing up and down, girl? No no, the women will like him the better for it won't they Sophie? (*Laughter.*) Come, sing us one of your jolly songs.

SOPHIE: Not now, father. I have a headache.

Western catches her, slapping her on the buttocks.

WESTERN: Let's have "Saint George he was for England," or "Bobbing Joan." That's a good one for you tonight, eh?

Camera pans Sophie to harpsichord. Western and Supple and Sophie. Sophie sits down. Western starts tapping away with his fork. Long shot: Sophie in foreground.

WESTERN: None of your old Handel now, my little darling.

She starts to play.

WESTERN: Ah, you play like an angel.

Sophie, furious, plays on.

LANE NEAR SEAGRIM'S BACKYARD. DAY.

Tom is riding along, preoccupied, grim. Camera tracking. He turns his horse off the road along a track through the woods.

COMMENTATOR: Molly's reputation was destroyed and Tom's heart was heavy with remorse. Perhaps Mr. Square had been right that the wicked were snared in the work of their own hands.

SEAGRIM'S BACKYARD.

Two of Mrs. Seagrim's daughters are working in the yard. Tom rides up and dismounts. Mrs. Seagrim appears.

MRS. SEAGRIM: Oh, Mr. Jones!

TOM: Where's Molly?

MRS. SEAGRIM (*obviously lying*): Oh, she? She ain't home.

Tom looks puzzled.

FIRST DAUGHTER (*spitefully*): She's upstairs, in bed!

Tom enters the cottage as Mrs. Seagrim throws stones at her daughter.

MOLLY'S GARRET ROOM.

This is built under the eaves of the cottage and we can see plainly the beams, straw and plaster of the roof. The room is in darkness. A loud knocking is heard outside the door.

MOLLY: Who is it?

TOM'S VOICE: It's me—Tom.

Molly slips back into her rumpled bed, pulling the clothes over her. Tom comes in, sheepishly.

MOLLY: Why haven't you been to see me before this, Tom?

TOM: Molly, I . . . I . . . Well . . .

MOLLY: Faugh! (*Taps her belly.*) I thought you said you'd be my gentleman.

Molly jumps up, standing on her bed. A chicken flies at Tom's face.

TOM: I hoped to explain why—

MOLLY: Oh you're not going to admit you've had your wicked will of me—

TOM: Molly—

She falls back on the bed. Tom is on his knees before her. She sobs magnificently, all over the bewildered Tom.

MOLLY: I shall never love any other man but you, Tom. Not if the greatest squire in the country were to come a-courting to me, I couldn't give myself to him. No, Tom, not for all the riches in the world, now that you've gained my heart. You are a lecherous rascal, after all, Tom. I shall always hate and despise the whole sex, and on account of you, Tom.

She is belting him with a pillow, flailing wildly, when a rug, nailed up against the rafters in service as a closet, collapses revealing Mr. Square, crouching with knees bent, head down, and quite naked—except for a nightcap belonging to Molly. Tom collapses with laughter. Molly collapses. The image is frozen.

COMMENTATOR: Mr. Square. Molly's favors after all had not been bestowed on Tom alone. Our hero unlike many other men was fortunate enough to discover the father of his child in time.

SOPHIE'S BEDROOM. DAY.

Mrs. Honor is gabbling at Sophie while she laces up her corsets as she dresses her for the hunt. Their faces are reflected in the mirror. Sophie pulls her dress over her head.

HONOR: And after everyone's kindness, too. She has laid the child at young Mr. Jones's door. All the parish say Mr. Allworthy is so angry with Mr. Jones that he won't see him. To be sure, one can't help pitying the poor young man. He is so pretty a gentleman, I should be sorry to see him turned out of doors.

SOPHIE: Why do you tell me all this? What concern have I in what Mr. Jones does?

HONOR: Why, ma'am, I never thought as it was any harm to say a young man was handsome. But I shall never think of him any more now. For handsome is as handsome does!

SOPHIE: Tittle tattle, tittle tattle. I shall be late for the hunt.

HONOR: Sorry, I'm sure, madam.

Honor leaves sullenly while her mistress bubbles with rage.

EXTERIOR. WESTERN'S HOUSE. DAY.

The hunt assembles in front of the house and gradually moves into the yard where the Western party's horses are being prepared. There is chaos everywhere as horses are saddled, hounds whipped in, stirrup cups drunk. Squire Western dominates the whole scene roaring welcomes to everyone and addressing the grooms and hounds. Tom expertly adjusts his own saddle and exchanges glances with Sophie. Blifil jumps out of the way for a batch of liverish colored hounds unleashed from the kennels.

(The whole of the meet will be shot in a loosish way packing each set-up with the maximum amount of incident and comedy business. The broad satirical comedy of contemporary prints.)

Among other lines, phrases overheard amidst the shouting and barking:

WESTERN (*examining a horse's teeth*): You're getting no younger.

TOM (*to Sophie*): You're not speaking today?

WESTERN: Drink up, Tom! Everybody! Health to everyone! (*Trying to pour a drink down a dog's mouth.*) Put a cider inside her. (*Clapping a woman on the buttocks and bending over her.*) Say, lassie, you'll have a Western . . .

TOM: Squire, it's too early. You'll tire yourself.

WESTERN: Huntsmen, loose the hounds!

THE HILL BEHIND WESTERN'S HOUSE.

The hounds are ready, the horses behind them.
Eyeline shot: A keeper among the trees sights a stag, he blows his horn. Panning shot: The hounds and the hunt are way up the hill and streaming through the trees. Panning shot: Two stags gallop up to the skyline, away into the valley beyond.

TOM: Come on, Sophie. Hurry!

THE HUNT.

Squire Western and Tom. Sophie rides along with them reluctantly, out of duty to her father. The hunt is no pretty Christmas calendar affair but a thumping dangerous vicious business, in which everyone takes part so wholeheartedly that it seems to express all in the raw, wild vitality that is so near to the surface of their lives. It is passionate and violent. Squire Western howls dementedly as he flogs his horse over the muddy earth. The curate kicks his beefy heels in the air, bellowing with blood and pleasure. Big, ugly, unlovable dogs tear at the earth. Tom reels and roars on his horse, his face ruddy and damp, almost insensible with the lust and the cry and the gallop, with the hot quarry of flesh in the crisp air, the blood and flesh of men, the blood and fur of animals. Everyone is caught up in the bloody fever. Admiration and desire scrawl their way around Sophie's eyes and mouth as she watches Tom.

(During the hunt itself the camera will always be in movement, either panning or tracking. There will be a great deal of close-up material, with the trees blurring the foreground, horses' heads sweating, hounds at full pelt, jumps, horses falling, the forward

eyeline of the stags. The camera will always be in motion to give the greatest feeling of speed and danger.)

Tracking: The hunt is spread out now and many riders have fallen behind. Only a small group led by Western and Tom, with Sophie's horse visible in the background, are up with the hounds. Hounds suddenly pick up a stronger scent. Tracking: The whole pack is off again. Tracking: Eyeline: The exhausted, dazed stag turns at bay as the first dog leaps for his throat. Tracking: Western urges his horse on. The hounds are tearing the stag to pieces. Western, Tom and three or four others thunder up and whip the dogs from the beast. With a great cry of triumph, Western holds up the carcass, streaming with blood, by the antlers. He thrusts it almost into the lens.

Sophie has just arrived at this terrifying sight. Her horse rears and rebels. She loses her bridle as the horse plunges away through the dark trees. Tom, who has dismounted, sees what has happened, leaps on his horse and gallops after her, camera panning with him. Tracking shot (long-focus lens): Sophie is a cool tough rider and she tries hard to control her horse. Side-angle tracking shot: Tom in pursuit. Side-angle tracking shot: Tom overtaking Sophie. He leaps down, grabs Sophie's bridle and the horse rears wildly and Sophie falls.

Tom lets go the bridle and breaks her fall by catching her in his arms. They both tumble to the ground and Tom covers her to protect her from the rearing hooves. Tom rolls over. Sophie is the first to recover. Tom is holding his left arm but he is the first to speak.

TOM: I trust you're not harmed.

SOPHIE: No, no—I am quite safe. How can I ever thank you, Mr. Jones?

TOM: If I have preserved you, madam, I am sufficiently repaid. (*He gasps in pain.*) Ah—ah!

SOPHIE (*concerned*): I hope you are not hurt.

TOM: If I have broken my arm, I consider it a trifle in comparison with what I have feared on your account.

SOPHIE: Broken your arm!

TOM (*rising*): I'm afraid I have, madam, yet I have another to lead you home.

Tom holds out his other arm. But then faints. Fade out. Fade in.

WESTERN'S HOUSE. TOM'S BEDROOM. DAY.

Tom is lying in bed asleep. Sophie is beside him watching. In the background Honor is laying out tea for Sophie on a small table. Outside the open window birds are singing.

HONOR: Look at him, ma'am, he's the most handsome man I ever saw in my life.

SOPHIE: Why, Honor, I do believe you're in love with him.

HONOR: I assure you, ma'am, I am not.

Mrs. Honor hands Sophie the cup of tea. Sophie turns and camera pans back to Tom as Sophie's line is overlaid. Tom opens his eyes.

SOPHIE (*softly*): If you were, I see no reason why you should be ashamed of it. For he is certainly a handsome fellow.

Tom looks at them quickly before they see him. His hand slides across the bed toward Sophie's hand.

HONOR: That he is, the most handsome man I ever saw in my life, and as you say, ma'am, I don't know why I should be ashamed of looking at him though he is my better.

Sophie and Honor, favoring Sophie. Unnoticed by Honor, Tom grasps Sophie's hand and she starts.

HONOR: For gentlefolk are but flesh and blood like us servants. I am an honest person's child, and my father and mother were married, which is more than some people can say, as high as they hold their heads.

Tom and Sophie's hands clench round each other, their knuckles turning white. Sophie almost gasps with pleasure.

Close-up: Sophie looks startled and tries to draw her hand away, thinking Honor has seen them, but Tom, his eyes still closed, won't let go. Close-up: Honor.

HONOR: My grandfather was a clergyman and he would have been very angry to have thought any of his family should have taken up with Molly Seagrim's leavings.

Close-up: Sophie. At this reminder, Sophie wrenches her hand away from Tom's. Tom opens his eyes.

HONOR: Why, ma'am, the young gentleman is awake!

SOPHIE: Yes, you've awakened him with all your foolish chatter.

TOM: I feel awake for the first time, madam.
Sophie blushes.

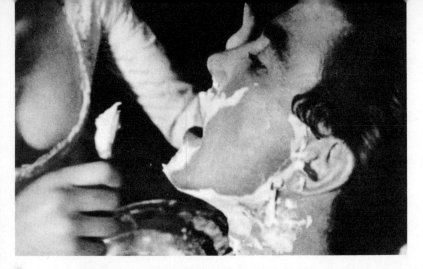

TOM'S CONVALESCENCE AND THE MENDING OF HIS ARM.

MONTAGE SEQUENCE. DAY.

INTERIOR. WESTERN'S. TOM'S BEDROOM.

EXTERIORS. HILL BEHIND WESTERN'S HOUSE. WESTERN'S GARDEN, LAKE AND BRIDGE.

Tom recovers gradually while Sophie takes charge. She shaves him. She rows him around the lake. She helps him on to his horse, etc. During the montage there is a growing sense of their

relationship and of Tom falling deeply in love with her. But it is not simply a straightforward idyllic relationship.

TOM (*reading to her while she pops candy in his mouth*): "To operate a narrow scru . . . narrow scrutiny, found some masquerade books, several vials of strange liquors, pots of ointment . . ."

Sophie is a very independent girl with a great sense of humor and determined to make the invalid play it her way. Finally, the splint is off Tom's arm.

LAKE. SQUIRE WESTERN'S.

Tom and Sophie walking with her pet dog. Camera tracking. When the dog returns with a ball Sophie has thrown, Tom picks it up to throw it. Tom laughs and throws the ball forcefully. They start to walk again and we continue to track.
Sophie blushes and turns away. Tom touches her neck. She turns and they kiss for the first time, half embarrassed.

HILLS.

Tom and Sophie ride joyfully together. Camera panning. Sophie gallops ahead and Tom chases her. He catches her up on the top of the hill. They stop. Surrounded by the sky they look over the rolling down, dappled with sunlight.

A COUNTRY ROAD. DAY.

In the distance we see a pony trap coming down a long hill. Suddenly, as it is nearing a corner down the hill, it takes on speed.

ALLWORTHY: Remember that picnic?

BRIDGET: How shall I ever forget? (*Suddenly alarmed.*) Brother! Brother!

ALLWORTHY (*pulling at the reins*): It's all right. Whoa! Whoa!

The pony has bolted and is beyond control. The trap is overturned into a ditch and the occupants hurled out. Allworthy and Mrs. Blifil lying in the ditch. Mrs. Blifil is seen by her staring eyes to be dead, her neck broken. The pony continues on its way.

ANOTHER COUNTRY ROAD.

Tom is joyously riding his horse, singing. At Allworthy's gatehouse he reacts to a strange sight.

EXTERIOR. ALLWORTHY'S HOUSE.

Blifil is standing outside with a group of anxious servants, and the remains of the trap which has been brought on a farm cart. Tom rides up.

TOM: Why the long face, Blifil?

BLIFIL: Such a terrible thing—

TOM: What—what's happened?

BLIFIL: There's been an accident. My mother is dead.

Tom jumps off his horse and joins Blifil, consoling him.

53

TOM: And Squire Allworthy?

BLIFIL: He's not expected to live.

Tom rushes past him into the house.

STAIRCASE.

Tom hurtles up the stairs. Thwackum is coming out of Allworthy's room.

THWACKUM: Sssh . . . Fever has developed, and there is little hope. We can only pray, something for which you have scant relish.

CHURCHYARD. DAY.

Coffin as it is lowered. It bears a plate with the inscription:

BRIDGET BLIFIL

BORN 12TH DECEMBER 1698

DIED 18TH JUNE 1749

Bells toll. Parson Supple, Squire Western, Sophie, Tom, Blifil, Thwackum, Square, etc., at the grave where the coffin is lowered.

SUPPLE: For as much as it has pleased Almighty God in His Great Mercy to take unto himself the soul of our dear sister, here departed, we therefore commit her body to the ground. Earth to earth, ashes to ashes, dust to dust, in sure and certain hope of the resurrection to eternal life, through our Lord, Jesus Christ.

CROWD: Amen!

WESTERN (*clapping on his hat*): Well, there's another one gone.

Blifil receives condolences. Tom's and Sophie's are silent.

WESTERN (*clapping Blifil on the arm*): Cheer up, lad.

THWACKUM: She will be with the angels, my boy.

SQUARE: Our mortal forms are but shadows of a purer reality.

BLIFIL (*to the parson*): Thank you, sir, for your comforting words.

SUPPLE: She was a great lady.

A shabby looking lawyer dressed in black, Dowling, approaches Mr. Blifil and they turn away from the grave.

DOWLING: Sir, some time before your mother died she gave me a letter. Her instructions were to hand it to Mr. Allworthy as she was buried.

BLIFIL: Hand it to me. I will hand it to my uncle.

DOWLING: She expressly said into no hands but Mr. Allworthy's.

BLIFIL: Lawyer Dowling, if my uncle lives, he will need a new steward. I intend to recommend you.

DOWLING: You are most kind, sir.

Dowling hands the letter over. Blifil goes off, tapping it. Iris in on Dowling.

ALLWORTHY'S BEDROOM. DAY.

Allworthy lies in bed, his breathing hard come by. Also in the room are Thwackum, Square, Blifil, a Lawyer, Footmen and other Servants. Blifil is blubbering rather theatrically.

ALLWORTHY (*to Blifil*): Do not grieve, my dear nephew, do not grieve.

TOM (*kneeling at the bedside*): Sir, you cannot die.

ALLWORTHY: Death comes to us all, Tom. (*He gasps.*) I have asked you here to tell you of my will. (*He motions to the lawyer.*) Nephew Blifil, I leave you the heir to my whole estate, with these exceptions: To you, my dear Tom, I have given an estate of £800 a year, together with £1000 in ready money.

Thwackum and Square exchange sour looks. Blifil scowls through his tears.

ALLWORTHY: I am convinced, my boy, that you have much goodness, generosity and honor in your nature. If you will add prudence and religion to these, you must be happy. One thousand pounds I leave to you, Mr. Thwackum, and a like sum to you, Mr. Square—which I am convinced exceeds your desires as well as wants. As for my servants, for Marjorie and Jane one hundred pounds. . . .

He groans and falls back on the pillows.

ALLWORTHY'S STUDY. DAY.

Blifil, Thwackum, Square and Dowling are sitting listening to Blifil reading the Bible with the curtains drawn against the daylight.

BLIFIL: ". . . My soul shall praise the Lord even unto death, and my life was drawing near to hell beneath. . . ."

There is a thunderous sound like a body falling downstairs.

ALLWORTHY'S HALL.

Tom comes roaring down the stairs, camera panning. The win-

*dows in the great hall are draped with black. With a wild gesture
of joy, Tom tears them down and the sunlight bursts in, flaring.
The others rush to the door. They stare at Tom in amazement.*

TOM: Mr. Allworthy's recovered! It's over! The fever has gone!
He is sitting up! He's well again! The Squire's recovered!

The flying drapes cover first the pious ones, then the screen.

*It is some hours later. Blifil, Thwackum and Square, Dowling,
and Tom are taking refreshment. Tom is very drunk and excited.*

COMMENTATOR: It is not true that drink changes a man's character. . . . It may reveal it more clearly. . . . The Squire's
recovery brought joy to Tom, to his tutors sheer disappoint-
ment. . . .

TOM (*singing*): Sing, thick Thwackum, your bounty's flown.

THWACKUM: You have a good reason for your drunkenness, you
beggarly bastard! He has provided well enough for you!

TOM (*rising and crossing to him*): You think any such considera-
tion could weigh with me? Damn you, Thwackum!

THWACKUM: How dare you, sir?

*Thwackum sits down, disgruntled, as Tom gets himself another
drink.*

TOM: Damn me if I don't open another bottle! (*laughs*) I shall sing you a ballad, a ballad which I have entitled "Sing Thick Thwackum, Your Bounty's Flown."

Tom sings. Blifil is drinking.

TOM: "Sing, Thick Thwackum, your bounty's flown. You've lost all the money you thought that you'd earned. . . ."

BLIFIL: Mr. Jones, the house is in mourning on account of the death of my dear mother.

TOM (*crosses to Blifil*): Oh sir, forgive me. My joy for Mr. Allworthy's recovery. . . .

He offers his hand, which Blifil refuses rudely.

BLIFIL: I had the good fortune to know who my parents were. Consequently I am grieved by their loss.

He gets up and makes for the door. Tom grabs Blifil by the collar.

TOM: You rascal! You dare insult me . . .

A brawl follows.

DOWLING: Gentlemen, gentlemen, this behavior is most unseemly.

Tom tries to punch Blifil, but Thwackum and Square are able to rescue Blifil and carry Tom to the door and throw him out.

EXTERIOR. ALLWORTHY'S FRONT ENTRANCE.

Tom lands in a heap, and picks himself up.

TOM: How dare you throw me out?

Blifil, Thwackum and Square on the terrace.

SQUARE: Shall we take the evening air?

ALLWORTHY'S GARDEN. NIGHT.

Tom, swinging along, stops to take a long swig from his bottle.

COMMENTATOR: It is widely held that too much wine will dull a man's desire. Indeed it will, in a dull man.

Tom stares up at the stars and sings. As he staggers away, his voice comes floating back in the still air. "Sophie." An ecstatic, tender roar of desire.

COUNTRYSIDE.

Tom stumbles about the fields and lanes bawling Sophie's name to the sky.

TOM: Sophie—Sophie—I'll carve her name on this tree. Tree, do you mind if I carve the name of my So-phie, Big S. S for Sophie. Sophie. So—

Tom is trying to carve the letter "S" into a tree, when the camera pans to Molly. Tom stares befuddled by the sight of her standing beside him with lots of her big white body showing beneath the filthy shift she works in.

TOM: M-M-Molly, Molly, Molly Molly Molly Molly. "M" for Molly

MOLLY (*laughs*): You aren't going to slit my throat, Squire?

TOM: Would you like a sip of my wine?

Tom hands her the wine bottle.

MOLLY: I've never sipped a gentleman's wine before (*She laughs and drinks and laughs again.*) It's very potent.

Tom giggles at camera. They both laugh. Tom doubles over with laughter, collapsing with it.

MOLLY: What are you laughing at, Tom?

TOM: I'm thinking of Square—in—in your bedroom.

After sharing this remembrance of Square for a while, Molly playfully kicks her foot at Tom's face on the ground. He grabs her dress and pulls her down into the tall grass. Laughing, they

roll over and over, disappearing with a dry crackle over a small slope. Camera holds discreetly on the slope.

COMMENTATOR: To those who find our hero's behavior startling, the answer is simple. Tom had always thought that any woman was better than none. While Molly never felt that one man was quite as good as two.

ALLWORTHY'S GARDEN, NEAR STREAM.

Blifil, Square and Thwackum are walking not a hundred yards away when they hear an exciting hunting shout, crossed with a cry as weighty as the sound of a mare being served. Which indeed is Molly being ridden happily and drunkenly by Tom.

SQUARE: He has a wench?

THWACKUM: A wench!

BLIFIL: A wench!

SQUARE (*shouting*): Let's go and find the wicked girl.

THWACKUM: Yes!

Blifil and Thwackum beat their way eagerly to the source of all this noisy rutting.

BEHIND HEDGE, ALLWORTHY'S GARDEN.

Two shot: Tom and Molly. Tom has only just time to get to his feet and adjust himself to the situation.

TOM: Who's that?

Camera looks with him, putting focus across the lawn where the three are running. Tom rushes to the plank across the tiny stream which the three are making for. Camera panning. He begins to struggle with them. Thwackum advances and tries to push Tom out of his way. Tom resists, and a fight ensues among the four men. It seems that Tom will lose after a while, for his arm is still painful. Blifil, Square and Thwackum are just forcing Tom to his knees when a figure appears. It is Squire Western.

WESTERN: Damnation to you. Stop it. Stop, what's the matter

with you? Damnation to you. You over there! 'Whoa there! Three falling onto one. Whoa! The whip.

As Sophie arrives, Blifil, Thwackum and Square have run off a distance.

WESTERN: Come, lass, see to Tom. He's in a devilish pickle, I promise you.

Sophie kneels beside him, wiping away the blood.

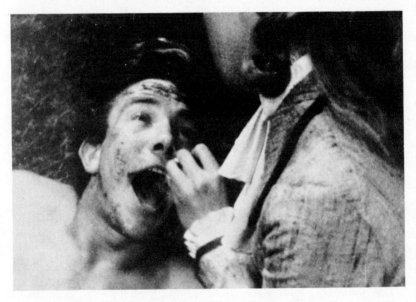

SOPHIE: Tom! Poor Tom. I'll fetch you some water.

Western kneels beside him.

WESTERN: What are you brawling about, Tom?

Sophie runs off. Blifil, Square and Thwackum are still some distance away.

THWACKUM: If you search the bushes you can find the reason.

WESTERN: Quarreling over a wench, eh?

Sophie dips her handkerchief in the stream. She sees Molly's leg. The two women exchange looks.

THWACKUM: Ask Mr. Jones, sir.

WESTERN: A wench! Ah! A wench! You lecherous dog!

Sophie returns. Western is beating around the bushes pretending to look for Molly, having a high old joke at Tom's expense.

WESTERN: Where is she? Where's Tom's pussy? Puss, puss, puss, puss, puss! Come, pussy.

TOM: Sophie, I—

Western is flogging this caper into the ground when Sophie suddenly gives Tom a hard slap with her wet handkerchief and storms off. Tom tries to follow her. Blifil and the tutors move in.

THWACKUM: Come, after him!

Western is trying to placate the others.

WESTERN: Tom, Tom, come and sup with me. And gentlemen, let us make our peace over a bottle.

THWACKUM: I beg your pardon. But it is no slight matter for a man of my character to be buffeted by a boy, just because I was trying to bring a wanton harlot to justice.

THWACKUM: The real fault lies in Mr. Allworthy and yourself, sir. If you would put the right laws in execution, you will soon rid the country of these vermin.

WESTERN: Hah! I would as soon rid the country of foxes!

Western hugs and kisses poor Tom and helps him onto his horse.

WESTERN: Come you, sup with me. Damn me, if there's nothing I won't give you—except my hounds . . . and my favourite mare! Up—Hah, hah. Away. Miss Slouch.

TOM: Hup there. Whoop.

They go off. Blifil and Thwackum glare after Tom and Western.

THWACKUM: Let us go and tell Mr. Allworthy how the monster has behaved.

BLIFIL: No, sirs, I beg of you. Let us wait. A better time will come.

EXTERIOR. WESTERN'S HOUSE. NIGHT.

Western, still laughing, rides up with Supple, Tom and Sophie.
Sophie is still livid and not speaking to Tom, who has to keep up
a front with Western. Camera pans them to the house. A coach
is drawn up outside.

WESTERN: Ods zodikins, it's me sister's coach? What brings her
from London? I hope the old bitch has gone to bed.

Laughter.

WESTERN'S HALL.

The party tumbles in, Western dragging Sophie by the arm.

WESTERN: Come, Sophie, sing us one of your jolly songs, my girl.

SOPHIE: Please, Father, I do not feel very well. I think I shall go to
bed.

WESTERN: Not before you attend to your guest. Tom has a great
thirst, I warrant you.

Seething, Sophie begins to fill pewter mugs from a great barrel
of ale. Tom hands them around and she glares at him. Western
is just about to propose a toast when there is a noise from the
minstrel gallery above. It is his sister, Miss Western. Miss Western,

Sophie's aunt, is very like her brother in temperament, although opposite in taste and habits. She is hot from hallooing it in the London salons. A likeable, downright blundering eighteenth-century Pen-Club lady. Nearly six feet tall and bent always on seeking out and solving complex problems, she is always blind to the simplest things. Miss Western is holding a candle. Camera looks up at her.

MISS WESTERN: Western, what are these nocturnal riots?

WESTERN: Now, lookee here, sister!

MISS WESTERN: Sophie!

SOPHIE: Yes, aunt?

MISS WESTERN: To bed!

WESTERN: Bed?

MISS WESTERN: Bed!

SOPHIE: I'd be glad to, madam.

Sophie goes obediently. Miss Western snorts down at her brother.

WESTERN: Now, lookee here, sister. . . .

MISS WESTERN: Brother, as I am here to stay a while, I shall sign a peace treaty with you—

WESTERN: Sister, I have often warned you not to talk the court gibberish to me.

MISS WESTERN: I pity your country ignorance from my heart.

WESTERN: And I despise your citified claptrap; I'd rather be anything than a courtier or a Presbyterian, or a crawler round those damned German kings, as I believe some people are.

MISS WESTERN: If you mean me, you know I am a woman—

WESTERN: Yes, and it's a good thing for you that you are. If you were a man, I'd have lent you a flick long ago! (*Laughs.*)

MISS WESTERN: Brother, I think you are a perfect goat. Good night sir.

She turns and goes. Western makes the sound of a goat.

WESTERN'S FARMYARD. DAY.

Miss Western steps determinedly through the farmyard. Camera tracking. It is milking time and cows are everywhere, as well as the usual mixture of pigs, geese, sheep, dogs, which always litter the back of the Western house. Miss Western is repelled by the filth and dung but nevertheless she has something on her mind and nothing will deter her, and any cow or pig in the way gets a sharp whack from her parasol. Eventually she finds her quarry, who is examining his great bull. Oblivious of the surroundings Miss Western plunges in.

MISS WESTERN: Brother! Brother! Brother! Brother, have you not noticed something very extraordinary about my niece Sophie lately?

WESTERN: Tell me, then, you know I love that girl more than my own soul.

MISS WESTERN: Well, unless I am deceived, my niece is desperately in love.

WESTERN (*explosively*): In love! In love! Without my consent! I'll disinherit her, and turn her out of doors stark naked without a farthing! Where is she?

He gives the bull a push in anger. It lumbers off. A milkmaid falls off a stool. Miss Western grabs him by the arm and steers him through the cows.

MISS WESTERN: Supposing she should have fixed on the very person you would have wished?

WESTERN: No, no. She can love who she pleases, but she'll marry the man I choose.

MISS WESTERN: But she has fixed on the very person you would have wished.

WESTERN: What?

MISS WESTERN: What think you of Mr. Blifil?

Western looks horror-struck for a moment.

WESTERN: Young Blifil?

MISS WESTERN: Well, who else could there be? In this rude country society who else is of her class?

WESTERN: Before George! Nothing could lie handier together as Allworthy's estate and mine. Sister, what would you advise me to do?

MISS WESTERN: I think you should propose the match to Mr. Allworthy immediately.

WESTERN: I will propose it. (*Calling out to a farm hand.*) Saddle my horse!

They go off, Miss Western pleased, the Squire flailing his whip.

ALLWORTHY'S GARDEN. DAY.

Allworthy and Blifil are waving goodbye to Western. He disappears on horseback through the gatehouse.

ALLWORTHY: Well, nephew, how do you feel about this marriage between yourself and Sophie Western?

BLIFIL: I shall do exactly as you wish, Uncle.

ALLWORTHY: Oh come, sir, that is a cold answer when confronted by the prospect of so beautiful a young lady.

BLIFIL: My dear uncle, I am well aware of the many pleasures of that noble institution, marriage, and I will gladly call upon the young lady at any time she would be pleased to receive me.

ALLWORTHY: Good, you shall call upon her this very afternoon.

They go off, Allworthy's hand on Blifil's shoulder.

WESTERN'S GARDEN. DAY.

Close shot of Miss Western looking around, almost at camera. She is on the rampage again and as soon as she spots her prey she marches off. Camera tracks with her, then she walks out of shot.

68

Sophie is sitting on the wooden seat, abstracted in the latest novel. Miss Western stalks up and plonks herself beside Sophie who quickly puts her book away.

MISS WESTERN: Sophie dear, what book is that you are reading?

SOPHIE: A sad one.

MISS WESTERN: You blush, my dear Sophie.

SOPHIE: I have no thoughts to be ashamed of.

MISS WESTERN: Now tell me, you know how I love you. You know the easiness of my nature. I have not always been like this, I used to be thought cruel—by the men I mean. I was called the cruel Parthenissa. Now come, Sophie, I've news that will delight you.

SOPHIE: News? What news, Aunt?

MISS WESTERN: This very afternoon your father has arranged for you to receive your lover.

SOPHIE (*rising*): My lover! He's coming! This afternoon!

MISS WESTERN: Yes, and you're to put on all your best airs.

SOPHIE (*lifting her up with both hands*): Why Aunt, you almost frighten me out of my senses!

MISS WESTERN: You will come to yourself again. He is a charming young fellow.

She smiles. Sophie is ecstatic.

SOPHIE: Oh, dear, dear Aunt. I know none with such perfections. So brave, and yet so gentle. So handsome! What matters his being base born?

Shooting over Sophie's shoulder on to Miss Western.

MISS WESTERN: Base born? What do you mean? Mr. Blifil base born!

Shooting over Miss Western's shoulder on to Sophie.

SOPHIE (*faintly*): Mr. Blifil!

MISS WESTERN: Mr. Blifil. Of whom else have we been talking?

SOPHIE: Why Mr. Jones!

MISS WESTERN: Mr. Jones!

SOPHIE: Mr. Blifil! You can't be in earnest! (*turning away*) Oh, then I am the most unhappy woman alive.

Miss Western now stands a few moments silent, while sparks of fiery rage flash from her eyes. At length, collecting all her force of voice, she thunders forth:

MISS WESTERN: How can you think of disgracing your family by allying yourself to a—a bastard?

SOPHIE (*lip trembling*): Madam, you have extorted this from me. Whatever were my thoughts of that poor unhappy Mr. Jones, I intended to carry them to the grave.

Sophie walks off. Miss Western snorts and stamps with rage. She snarls after Sophie.

MISS WESTERN (*shouting*): I would rather follow you to that grave than see you disgrace us by such a match.

Sophie, who has stopped, turns and walks off swiftly.

EXTERIOR. WESTERN'S STABLE. DAY.

Terrified pigs scatter from a trough overturned by an enraged Western. Camera pans to a close shot of Sophie. She is pleading with her father and the whole farmyard is in an uproar as he lays about him with a riding crop.

WESTERN: Yes! Yes!

SOPHIE: No, no, no, no, no, I will not marry that idiot! To force me to do so would be to kill me!

WESTERN: Then die and be damned!

Shooting toward house, panning: Sophie squeals and rushes away from Western, almost knocking into Tom who has just ridden up. His horse rears and he is bewildered by the tremendous uproar. Western sits himself on a bale of hay, seething.

WESTERN: Damn me, what a misery it is to have daughters when a man has a good mare and dogs. Tom, that pig-headed hussy dares to refuse to marry Mr. Blifil. I'll turn her penniless out of doors if she doesn't. Go to her, lad, and see what you can do.

Tom dismounts and follows Sophie. Western pitches his ale in the face of a nearby bulldog.

IN FRONT OF WESTERN'S HOUSE.

Sophie is running.

MISS WESTERN: Sophie, Sophie, Sophie, Sophie, Sophie.

Miss Western is just passing by when Sophie, seeing her aunt, rushes away sobbing wildly. Miss Western stares after her. Tom rushes up in pursuit, shouting:

TOM: Sophie!

Miss Western tries to intercept him. He doesn't notice her. Frustrated she glares, then yelling:

MISS WESTERN: No, no, no! Brother! Brother! Brother!

She charges off to the stables. Cows being driven out of the yard engulf her.

WESTERN'S LAKE.

Tom sees Sophie sobbing by a tree at the side of the lake. We pan him to kneel. He comforts her. The scene is shot very close. She lifts her eyes presently, as he lifts her to her knees.

TOM: Sophie, Sophie, Sophie, my dearest. Promise me that you won't give yourself to Blifil.

SOPHIE: Don't say that name to me.

TOM: Tell me—tell me I may hope.

SOPHIE: Tom, you must go.

TOM: Sophie, please.

SOPHIE: You'll be destroyed.

TOM (*simply*): The only destruction I fear—is the loss of my Sophie. I cannot part with you.

She cannot withdraw her hand and they can scarcely move for fear of trembling. They clasp each other desperately.

72

Western is still seated. Mr. Supple is on hand.

MISS WESTERN: Can't I make you understand, you country clod?

WESTERN: Tom Jones! (*jumping up, spilling ale on his sister*) Damnation! Where is he? That home wrecker!

MISS WESTERN: There they are.

They run off.

WESTERN'S GARDENS AND LAKE.

Squire Western appears and, following the Squire, are Miss Western and Mr. Supple. We pan them to Tom and Sophie.

SOPHIE: Tom, you must go! Run, Tom, run!

The Squire has to be pinioned by the parson to stop him assaulting Tom. Sophie and Supple tell Tom to flee as Supple cannot hang on to the old lunatic. Western roars after Tom and we pan as he departs across the bridge.

WESTERN: I'll get thee, if I hang for it.

SOPHIE: Tom! Run!

The other side of the lake. Tom stops and turns. Tom's eyeline of Sophie being dragged off by Western and Miss Western. Tom turns and walks disconsolately.

ALLWORTHY'S DRIVE.

Squire Western comes charging up the great avenue of beech trees and bursts in to interrupt Allworthy and Blifil.

WESTERN: You there, Allworthy! A fine piece of work you've done!

ALLWORTHY (*rising*): What can be the matter, Mr. Western?

Western begins to dismount.

WESTERN: My daughter has fallen in love with your *bastard*. That's what comes of trying to bring up a bastard like a gentleman, and letting him go round visiting to nice folks' houses.

He leads the horse with him to the group of chairs on the lawn.

ALLWORTHY: I am sorry to hear you say this.

WESTERN: A pox on your sorrow. I have lost my only daughter, my poor Sophie, the joy of my heart.

He slumps in a chair. Allworthy and Blifil exchange looks.

WESTERN: Little did I think when I loved him for a sportsman that he was all the while a-poaching after my daughter.

He sits slumped in misery. His horse has wandered off and is eating the flowers. Allworthy retrieves the horse. Blifil hurries to help. Western downs a big drink.

ALLWORTHY: I wish you had not given him so many opportunities with her.

WESTERN: What the devil did she have to do with him? He came a-hunting with me, not a-courting to her.

ALLWORTHY: What are we to do, Mr. Western?

WESTERN: Keep the rascal away from my house till I lock the wench up. I'll make her marry Mr. Blifil if it's the last thing I do.

Western goes to Mr. Blifil who is rather ineffectually holding the horse by the path.

WESTERN (*shaking Blifil by the hand*): I'll have no other son-in-law but you. Go to her, you jolly dog! I tell you, you shall have her. (*He mounts the horse.*) And as for that son-of-a-

whore Jones, if I catch him anywhere near my girl, I'll qualify him to run for the gelding's plate! Come on, old Slouch, come on.

Western starts to ride off. The horse twists round and Western lands in the bushes.

COMMENTATOR: Even the best of horsemen should avoid the bottle.

ALLWORTHY'S HOUSE. STAIRCASE. NIGHT.

Thwackum, followed by Square and Blifil, descend the stairs.

COMMENTATOR: However, the forces of sobriety were gathering in all their strength against our hero.

With sad patience, Allworthy listens to Tom's accusers, who delight in their malicious accusations.

THWACKUM (*to Allworthy*): We call your attention to the abominable behavior of Mr. Jones.

SQUARE: He is a monster of depravity and should be expelled from your house this instant.

Allworthy turns away.

WESTERN'S FIELD. DAY.

It is hay-making time and like many of his contemporaries, Squire Western is not above taking a hand with his laborers. A great cart is being loaded and Squire Western is perched on top, forking the hay handed from below. Miss Western has just burst in on him and the argument is in full swing with the two of them bawling in the summer air.

WESTERN: You let her out of her room! After I locked her in?

MISS WESTERN: Women are convinced by reason, not by force.

WESTERN: The English of which is: I am in the wrong.

MISS WESTERN: As soon as she came back to live with you, brother, she imbibed these romantic notions.

WESTERN: You don't imagine, do you, that I taught her such things!

MISS WESTERN: Your ignorance, brother, as the great Milton says, almost subdues my patience.

She sweeps off among the gawping laborers.

WESTERN: Damn Milton! If he had the impudence to be here and say so to my face, I'd lend him a flick!

Western waves his fork at his vanishing sister. He claps one of the farm girls on the buttocks and falls into the hay on top of her.

WESTERN: Oh, come on, my girl.

The farm girl screams.

ALLWORTHY'S STUDY. NIGHT.

Allworthy is seated in a chair by his table. Thwackum and Square are crowding around him. In every camera set-up in the next scenes they must hem him in, bear down on him as if it were impossible for Allworthy to escape the accusations they are making. Thwackum and Square are at their most belligerent. Blifil is at his most hypocritical.

THWACKUM: He was, according to the vulgar phrase, whistle drunk.

SQUARE: On the very day of your utmost danger, he filled the house with riot and debauchery. And he even struck Master Blifil.

ALLWORTHY: How! Did he dare strike you?

Camera pans Blifil to Allworthy after he has exchanged glances with the others. Blifil is seated.

BLIFIL: Oh, Uncle I'm sure I have forgiven him that long ago.

Allworthy nods approvingly.

BLIFIL (*rising*): But the same evening we unluckily saw him with a girl in a manner not fit to be mentioned!

Allworthy turns, shocked. Thwackum and Square nod in confirmation.

BLIFIL (*continues*): Mr. Thwackum advanced to rebuke him, when, I am sorry to say it, he fell upon the worthy man, and beat him outrageously.

Allworthy sighs.

WESTERN'S GARDEN. DAY.

Sophie is picking peas. She is trying to avoid a battle with her aunt, but Sophie's exasperation builds throughout the scene.

MISS WESTERN: Tell me, child, what objections can you have to the young gentleman?

SOPHIE: A very solid objection, in my opinion. I hate him.

MISS WESTERN: Well, I have known many couples, who have entirely disliked each other, lead very comfortable, genteel lives.

SOPHIE (*turns*): Madam, I assure you I shall never marry a man I detest.

Miss Western, more furious than ever, marches back to her brother again.

ALLWORTHY'S STUDY. NIGHT.

Later. The three monsters have been steadily grinding away.

ALLWORTHY: I still believe the young man to have a few redeeming graces. Some of the crimes you accuse him of really sprang from his mistaken compassion to the gamekeeper and his family.

Square leaps in like a tiger.

SQUARE: Compassion, sir. Lust. All his gifts, his so-called generosity, were bribes to debauch another innocent—as you know —the unfortunate Molly . . .

THWACKUM: Miss Sophie Western will be the next to be undone. All this I would have revealed long ago had not Master Blifil begged me to give him another chance.

Close shot: Allworthy looks at Blifil. Close-up: Blifil looks suitably pained. Square and Thwackum are implacable. Allworthy rises.

ALLWORTHY: Send him to me.

Later. Long shot, high angle: Tom and Allworthy alone.

ALLWORTHY: Tom, I have forgiven you too often in the past out of compassion for your youth and in hope of your improvement. You must leave my house forever. However, I have educated you like my own child and would not turn you naked into the world. Here is something which will enable you with industry to get a good employment.

Close shot: Tom's reaction.

Close shot: Allworthy.

ALLWORTHY: Good-bye, Tom.

Allworthy turns to go. Close shot of Tom.

Long shot, high angle: Tom alone in the room.

EXTERIOR. ALLWORTHY'S HOUSE. DAWN.

Tom and a group of tearful servants are saying their goodbyes. Tom walks sadly away. Camera tracks on Tom's back until in the forecourt, he turns and looks back at the house he has lived in for twenty years. His hunting dog wants to accompany him.

TOM: Stay, boy. Stay.

Long shot: Tom's eyeline of Allworthy's house. The servants wave to him with handkerchiefs, Tom with his walking stick. Tom turns away and sets out alone down Allworthy's avenue of trees.

EXTERIOR. WESTERN'S HOUSE. DAY.

Sophie and Blifil walking in the gardens, Miss Western watching at a distance.

80

BLIFIL: Mr. Allworthy is very sensible of the many advantages of binding our two estates together.

SOPHIE: Indeed? I had not realized that Mr. Allworthy was so interested in questions of property.

BLIFIL: Oh, he is.

SOPHIE: And you?

BLIFIL (*puffing*): I? Well, naturally, my attention is set constantly on those most blissful and ah—sanctified—pleasures of holy matrimony.

He moves into her, but she turns aside. Enter Miss Western.

MISS WESTERN (*waggish*): Clandestine amours so soon Mr. Blifil!

SOPHIE: I pray you, Aunt, excuse me. I feel a little faint.

She goes out. Miss Western pats Blifil.

MISS WESTERN: The fox, Mr. Blifil! The fox! Tallyho!

Blifil nods and follows Sophie while Miss Western beams.

BACK OF WESTERN'S GARDEN. BELOW TOWER.

It is late afternoon and the work has stopped while kitchen maids serve food and great flagons of scrumpie. Western is lying in the hay with a farm girl beside him. Miss Western descends again.

MISS WESTERN: It is you who has taught her disobedience, brother. You are such a boor.

WESTERN: Boar! I am no boar! No, nor an ass!

Western props himself up enough to down a draft of ale.

MISS WESTERN: Oh more than Gothic ignorance. As for your manners, they deserve a cane.

WESTERN: And yours, madam, I despise as much as I do a fart.

There is a loud farting noise as Squire Western rolls on top of the farm girl.

Miss Western is astounded, and begins to leave. The Squire staggers to his feet.

WESTERN: And as for your niece, madam, I'm going to lock her up in my tower this time.

MISS WESTERN: You'll do nothing of the sort.

Western staggers after her, but stumbles and falls over a pile of hay.

WESTERN'S GARDENS. DAY.

Sophie is plotting with Honor, who is trembling with fright.

SOPHIE: Honor, you must promise to keep your word.

HONOR: I can't madam. I'm frightened. I can't.

She cries away, which seems to harden Sophie with resolve.

Squire Western lurches toward them carrying a pitchfork.

WESTERN: Ah, ah! Got you, my girl!

Sophie screams.

WESTERN: Come on. You won't get out this time, I warrant you.

He drags her toward the tower in the background. Miss Western storms up furiously. Honor blubbers.

COUNTRY ROAD. DAY.

Tom is tramping rather wearily along a chalk road and as he turns downhill, the camera pans with him to reveal a company of Redcoats, bivouacking by the roadside.

COMMENTATOR: Our hero was now on the road to London. His first adventure was with a party of those men whose profligate ways could be conducted with safety only under the protection of their Redcoats.

Tom approaches the group.

TOM: Good day, gentlemen, may I ask where you are heading?

SERGEANT: We're going north to fight for the Protestant cause.

TOM: Against Prince Charles?

SERGEANT: Yes, those damned Scots are already on their way to England.

TOM: I've been walking all day and am very hungry. May I buy something to eat and drink?

The soldiers, at once sensing his liberality, give him bread and cheese in exchange for some coins.

SERGEANT: Right. Give him some.

TOM: Thank you.

The Lieutenant, who has been watching the scene, gets up and we pan him toward Tom.

TOM: Good day, Captain.

LIEUTENANT: Good day. I see you are a gentleman. We shall be glad to welcome any such into our company.

TOM (*shaking his hand*): I'd be glad to march with you.

LIEUTENANT: Good. We shall be on the march in a short while.

One of the officers eyes him skeptically.

ROAD TO LONDON. DAY.

Tracking with Tom, marching and drinking with the soldiers. On the march the soldiers sing "Rule Britannia."

INTERIOR. GEORGE INN. NIGHT.

Here Tom has a rousing noisy dinner with some of the officers. The Lieutenant who has befriended Tom is a very sober, correct man. With them is an aggressive ensign named Northerton. When he fails to get his hand in the Landlady's decollatage, he whacks her on the rump. She goes round the table and lifts one of the servants off a soldier's lap.

COMMENTATOR: There 'comes a time when men in a constant state of readiness for war will slip their leash and fight like dogs.

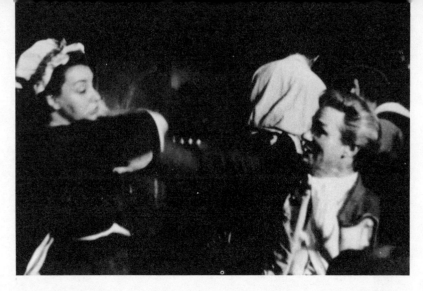

Camera tracks in to a closer shot of Tom. He is rather drunk.

TOM: I believe that a man can fight for no nobler cause than that of his religion.

ALL MEN: Hear, hear.

TOM: I'd like to drink a toast to the Protestant cause.

ALL MEN: The Protestant cause.

Close shot Adderly (another ensign), panning to Northerton.

ADDERLY: Smoke the prig out, Northerton, smoke him.

NORTHERTON: Sir, were you ever at university?

Tom realizes he is being got at.

TOM: Sir, so far from having been at university, I was never at school.

LANDLADY: Me neither.

NORTHERTON: I presumed, sir, only upon the information of your great learning.

TOM: Sir, it's as easy for a man not to have been at school and know something as it is for a man to have been at school and know nothing.

Laughter.

LIEUTENANT: Well said, young volunteer. Upon my word, Northerton, you had better let him alone or he'll prove too hard for you. Give us a toast, young fellow. Fill up his cup.

Glasses are filled and camera pans with Tom as he rises to give a toast.

TOM: I would like to propose a toast to the health, and bless the name of—Miss Sophie Western.

ALL MEN: Sophie Western.

NORTHERTON (*taking a sniff of snuff*): I know one Sophie Western was lain with by half the young fellows at Bath! Perhaps this is the same woman.

Tom won't be drawn at first.

TOM: Miss Western is a young lady of great fashion and fortune.

NORTHERNTON: Aye, aye, and so she is. It is the same young lady. I'll lay half a dozen of Burgundy that Tom French of our regiment had her in the tavern at Bridge Street.

There is a great roar of laughter from the whole group. Tom starts to lose his sense of humor.

TOM: Sir, I can bear no jesting with this lady's character.

Northerton rises, slightly drunk.

NORTHERTON: Jesting! Damn me if I was ever more in earnest in my life. Tom French of our regiment had both her and her aunt together at Bath.

TOM: Then I must tell you that you are one of the most impudent rascals on earth.

At which Northerton picks up a bottle and hurls it at Tom's head.
Camera pans up with bottle and there is a bellow as it flies, hurled by Northerton, at Tom's head. He goes down like a stone.
Northerton is laughing.

LANDLADY: You've killed him, you swine.

Northerton starts to excuse himself.

NORTHERTON: Zounds! I was but in jest with the fellow. I never heard of Miss Western before in my life.

LIEUTENANT: Then you deserve to be hanged. You are under arrest. Sergeant, take him away.

SERGEANT: Arrest him!

Three soldiers come forward to take custody of Northerton. One of them is later to act as the sentinel. Before leaving the room with his prisoner, the sentinel casts a sorrowful look at Tom whom he naturally supposes to be dead. Tom's limp body is picked up by the others. The image freezes.

COMMENTATOR: But a hero cannot be lost before his tale is told. For heaven be thanked we live in such an age when no man dies for love except upon the stage.

GEORGE INN. BEDROOM. NIGHT.

Camera pulls back to reveal the room: Tom, looking extremely pallid, his light-colored coat covered in blood, his head heavily bandaged, looks like bloody Banquo as he wakes up and raises himself from the bed.

He takes up the lighted candle, softly opens the door, and issues forth in pursuit of Northerton. There is a sword in the room left by one of the soldiers which Tom picks up.

TOM: I'll kill you, Northerton. I'm going to kill you, Northerton. Northerton, I must find Northerton. I must find Northerton. Northerton! Northerton!

INN YARD.

The sentinel guards the archway to the inn. He is sleeping. Tom appears, a ghostly figure in his nightshirt, with candle and sword.

90

He starts to descend. Tom yells.

TOM: Northerton! Northerton!

The sentinel wakes up. His hair begins to lift his Grenadier's cap, his knees knock together.

SENTINEL: Help! Help! The ghost walks.

His whole body contorted, he fires his rifle and falls flat on his face.

EXTERIOR. SQUIRE WESTERN'S HOUSE. NIGHT.

From a window Sophie throws out a ladder composed of knotted sheets and slides down it; after having first thrown down a bundle of belongings. The hounds in their kennels stir and growl; Sophie quiets them and their noise quickly subsides as they recognize their mistress.

WESTERN'S HALL.

Squire Western snoring like a ruptured dragon; his dogs lying at his feet sound as if they are sleeping it off too.

BEDROOM.

Miss Western wakes with the noise from outside.

EXTERIOR. WESTERN'S STABLES.

Sophie quietly leads her horse out of the stables, whispering as she saddles it. Honor's terror has reduced her to impotence. Sophie puts her on the horse and leads it out.

BEDROOM.

Miss Western goes back to sleep.

EXTERIOR. WESTERN'S HOUSE.

Sophie mounts and they set off down the street along the clear moonlit road to London. A cock crows; the sound continues over cut to next scene.

The next morning. Sunlight is streaming in through the windows. The Landlady is shaking Tom.

LANDLADY: Come on, you, get up. I can't afford for you to lie here any longer. Get out and follow those rascally friends of yours. You soldiers call yourselves gentlemen. But it's we who have to pay for you. And keep you too, for that matter.

TOM: What are you talking about?

LANDLADY (*pulling the bedclothes off him*): That Lieutenant Northerton escaped last night, and the rest of the company went in pursuit of him, and they very conveniently left here without paying the bill.

TOM: Well, how could he have escaped?

LANDLADY: His doxie arrived, a trollop called Mrs. Waters. The sentry had disappeared, and she let him out. But she'll soon learn what kind of a man he is. Nothing is ever good enough for sparks like him, but when it comes to paying the bill, that's another matter.

TOM: Don't worry, madam. I will repay you handsomely.

Tom staggers out of bed and searches his trousers for money.

LANDLADY: A nice young gentleman like yourself shouldn't want to get mixed up with these rough soldiers.

TOM: It's gone!

LANDLADY: What's gone?

TOM: I had a £500 note in my breeches, and it's gone.

LANDLADY: That's a likely story.

TOM: I had £500 . . .

LANDLADY: You never had £500 . . .

Both argue and shout. In the midst of the yelling Tom turns to the camera.

TOM: Did you see her take that £500?

LANDLADY: You lying rascal—nor your cheating redcoat friends either—go on take your things and get out of here. Quick, go on. I'll set the dogs on you if you don't hurry up. The blackguard. Robber. The whole lot of you and your five hundred pounds.

GEORGE INN COURTYARD.

The landlady throws his belongings after him. He catches his walking stick neatly and leaves the George Inn in gay spirits, humming a tune as he marches along.

SQUIRE WESTERN'S HALL. DAY.

Squire Western is asleep, still littered with dogs. Miss Western enters in her traveling clothes. She belts the dogs and thumps the Squire.

MISS WESTERN: Wake up, you country stewpot!

WESTERN: What!

MISS WESTERN: Your daughter, sir. While you've been lying a-bubbling here your daughter is gone! Rouse yourself from this pastoral torpor! Your daughter is gone!

The Squire casts her a baleful glance.

EXTERIOR. WESTERN'S HOUSE.

Squire Western rides up, yelling back to his sister in her coach. Parson Supple accompanies on another horse. They ride off.

WESTERN: What ... Come on, you lazy lout, and take the London road. Come on, me Slouch.

GEORGE INN COURTYARD. DAY.

Sophie and Honor arrive on their horse.

LANDLADY: Are you wanting anything, madam?

94

SOPHIE: We're tired after a long journey and in need of some refreshment.

LANDLADY: It'd be an honor to serve such a lady. Let me help you down.

SOPHIE: Has by any chance a young gentleman, a Mr. Jones, passed this way lately?

LANDLADY: Indeed he has, madam. And I'm surprised at a lady like you inquiring of the likes of him. Brawling, thieving and bragging about his mistress, one Miss Sophie Western.

SOPHIE: Sophie Western?

HONOR: I'm not at all surprised, madam, after that Molly Seagrim.

SOPHIE: But I am the same Sophie Western.

LANDLADY: Well, you can get out of here quick and take your trollop with you. Go on, get out of here. Follow your fine friends and take your fine airs and graces with you.

All three are shouting at each other, as the horse and riders leave.

LANDLADY: Go on, we don't want the likes of you here.

WOODS. DAY.

Tom marching along cheerfully.

COMMENTATOR: Our hero's next adventure concerns a lady in circumstances from which any gentleman would instinctively wish to free her. But of which any man who was not a gentleman might instantly want to take advantage.

As Tom approaches camera, a shout is heard. He stops. Eyeline shot of the exposed roots of a tree on the hillside. An oddly erotic scene of a half-naked woman being rather unaccountably tied up with a garter by Northerton. He is trying to hang her.

TOM: Let her go, you villain! You savage!

Pan with Tom rushing at Northerton who escapes down the hill.

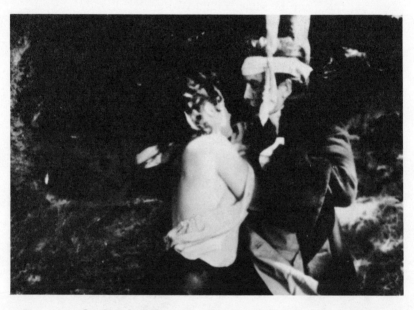

Tom turns back to cut down the woman. The woman, Mrs. Waters, raising her hands to cover her breasts, smiles at Tom. Northerton returns and does battle with Tom. Sword versus walking stick. When Tom has gained the advantage he seems on the point of thrusting the sword into the prone Northerton. Instead he plants

it between the ensign's legs where it swings mockingly. Mrs. Waters, who has been terrified, smiles again.

Northerton runs off as Tom goes to Mrs. Waters. He unties her hands. She doesn't appear in the slightest disconcerted by her half nakedness—rather delighted to have a savior like Tom. Tom is embarrassed by the situation and takes off his coat to offer it to her.

MRS. WATERS: Surely, I've only myself to blame for putting my trust in a man so unworthy of my favors. No, indeed, sir, you've already had trouble enough. My nakedness might well make me ashamed, and I'd go alone, if it wasn't for the need of your protection.

Mrs. Waters smiles again and camera crabs around her as from Tom's eyeline. Tom is fascinated, but getting a little hot.

TOM: Well, then—in case any prying eyes should offend you, I will walk ahead, and escort you as far as Upton.

COMMENTATOR: So Tom and Mrs. Waters, for so the lady was called, set out on the road to Upton. Tom like Orpheus leading Eurydice out of hell, hardly daring to look back in case the fires consumed him.

Tracking with Tom marching ahead. He can't resist looking back.

Tracking with Mrs. Waters. She smiles.

Tracking with Tom, who turns ahead. He reacts to the peering eye of the camera, doffs his hat and covers the camera with it.

Panning shot: Sophie and Honor on their horse on the road. A coach appears behind them, then overtakes. A head appearing from one of the windows. It is Mrs. Fitzpatrick. She is only a little older than Sophie, a little more sophisticated, less pretty. Mrs. Fitzpatrick's eyeline, tracking.

MRS. FITZPATRICK: Sophie! Sophie Western! Sophie, cousin Sophie!

HONOR: La, ma'am, it's Mrs. Fitzpatrick!

SOPHIE: My cousin, Harriet?

HONOR: The same.

SOPHIE: Why, so it is.

Mrs. Fitzpatrick stops her coach and runs from it to Sophie, who has dismounted.

MRS. FITZPATRICK: Cousin! What are you doing here?

SOPHIE: I'm on my way to London.

MRS. FITZPATRICK: That's my destination. But why are you both on one horse indeed?

SOPHIE: Oh, Harriet, I am running away from home.

Mrs. Fitzpatrick laughs.

MRS. FITZPATRICK: I too! Running away from my husband, Mr. Fitzpatrick, who's hot on my trail, I'm sure. Oh, never marry an Irishman, particularly if he is eaten up with jealousy, and possessed of a quick temper, and a mighty fool into the bargain!

SOPHIE: But cousin, what will you do alone in London?

Harriet Fitzpatrick becomes a little coy.

MRS. FITZPATRICK: I have a friend. He has taken lodgings for me in Curzon Street.

Sophie laughs.

SOPHIE: Cousin.

MRS. FITZPATRICK: He is a dear kind man, and a peer of the realm. You can stay with me.

SOPHIE: Oh, may I?

MRS. FITZPATRICK: Come on.

SOPHIE: But your friend.

MRS. FITZPATRICK (*quickly changing the subject*): Oh, he is away for a few days, but when he returns we shall make other arrangements. Now get in, cousin, get in and tell me about yourself.

Sophie climbs in.

Long shot: The coach with Honor following behind disappears over the skyline, camera panning. We hear their voices die away chattering girls' talk.

EXTERIOR. THE INN AT UPTON.

Tom and Mrs. Waters arrive in the courtyard, camera pans to landlord and his wife. Their smiles fade, at the unusual sight presented to them. The lawyer Dowling covers his face with his hat.

TOM (*to Hostess*): Landlady, two rooms, please. And perhaps

you would be so good as to find this lady a gown. She's been involved in an accident and deprived of her clothes. Take us to our rooms at once.

Tom carries off the whole situation with the greatest aplomb. Camera holds on landlady and landlord, who mutter sullenly to each other.

Tom and Mrs. Waters go to the inner courtyard of the tavern. Susan, the chambermaid, is beating a rug. Tom and Mrs. Waters follow Susan upstairs. Iris in on Dowling, watching.

DINING ROOM. NIGHT.

Tom eats a tremendous eighteenth-century type meal while Mrs. Waters watches him, obviously entranced with him. As his appetite is slowly satisfied, so she gets to work on him, and his eyes and attention slowly shift from his food to her.

Two shot of Tom and Mrs. Waters.

COMMENTATOR: Heroes, whatever high ideas we may have of them are mortal not divine. We are all as God made us and many of us much worse.

Sequence of close shots of Tom as he drinks and eats, getting more and more transfixed by Mrs. Waters.

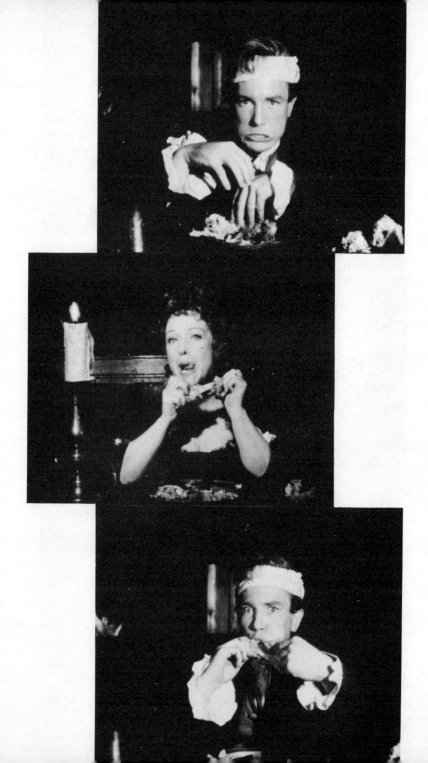

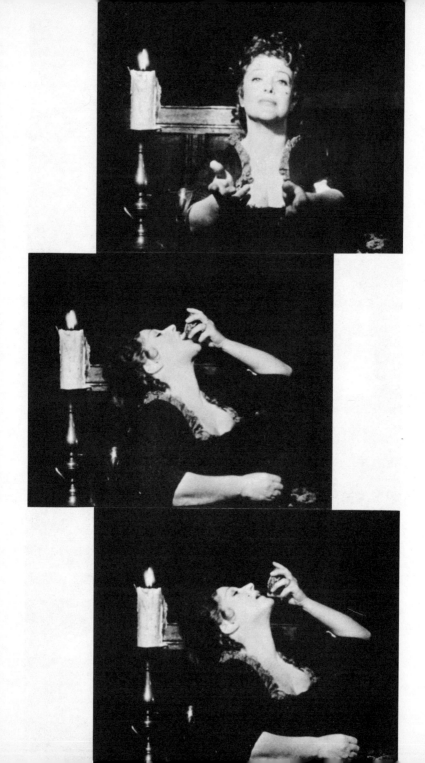

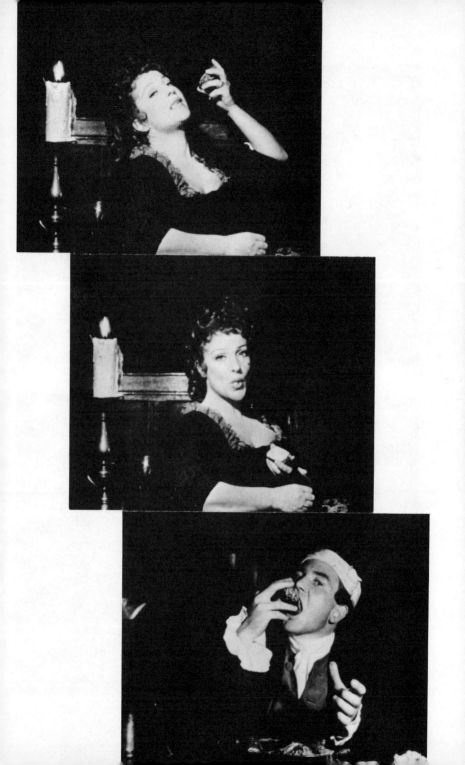

CORRIDOR.

Along the corridor toward the bedroom come the lurching figures of Tom and Mrs. Waters. They almost fall through the door into the bedroom.

MRS. WATERS' BEDROOM.

The warm flash of a candle flame across the bed. A giggle. The door closes. Tom and Mrs. Waters kiss. He pinches out the candle. Darkness.

116

OUTER COURTYARD.

There is a furious banging from outside the door. Wearily, Susan, the chambermaid, goes to open it.

SUSAN: All right, all right. I'm coming, I'm coming, I said.

She finds facing her, Mr. Fitzpatrick, an enraged, daft Irishman. He is panting hard. Camera tracks with Mr. Fitzpatrick; Susan follows.

FITZPATRICK: Where's me wife?

SUSAN: Who?

FITZPATRICK: Me wife, Mrs. Fitzpatrick. Where is she? I've come a distance to catch her.

SUSAN: There's no Mrs. Fitzpatrick here.

FITZPATRICK: I know she's here. I know it.

Mr. Fitzpatrick moves out of shot and camera holds on Susan.

INNER COURTYARD.

Tracking with Mr. Fitzpatrick. Susan joins him. They stop.

FITZPATRICK: Who's here, girl? (*He takes out a handful of guineas.*) Tell me who's here, and I'll make you the richest poor woman in the nation.

SUSAN: Nay, sir, there's only a gentleman, Mr. Jones—

FITZPATRICK: No lady?

SUSAN: He has a Mrs. Waters with him.

FITZPATRICK: Waters! I'll bet she's using a false name.

SUSAN: Eh?

FITZPATRICK: Cunning wench. Beside the waters of Babylon I shall lay me down. I'll bet she's laying down beside Mr. Jones. Show me her room!

Susan is intimidated by his mad manner. They move to the flight of steps in the inner courtyard which leads upstairs.

OUTER COURTYARD.

A coach rolls up and from it alight Sophie and Mrs. Fitzpatrick. Honor is with them. They look around, puzzled at finding the place empty and deserted.

UPSTAIRS CORRIDOR.

FITZPATRICK: Now where is she?

SUSAN: I'll show you.

Tracking with Susan and Fitzpatrick, Susan nods at the door in front of them.

FITZPATRICK (*yells*): Mrs. Fitzpatrick. Come on, Mrs. Fitzpatrick.

INNER COURTYARD AT FOOT OF STEPS.

Sophie and Mrs. Fitzpatrick have come through the inner courtyard. They are rather bewildered.

MRS. FITZPATRICK: My husband!

SOPHIE: Your husband?

MRS. FITZPATRICK: Mr. Fitzpatrick! Do you think I don't know his voice.

MRS. WATERS' BEDROOM.

Fitzpatrick kicks open the door.

FITZPATRICK: Discovered!

By the candlelight, Tom can be seen quite clearly in bed with Mrs. Waters, who dives beneath the clothes. Tom jumps out of bed as Fitzpatrick charges into the room. As they grapple Susan escapes from the room and dashes along the corridor. Mrs. Waters' voice can be heard screaming, "Help! Murder! Rape! Rape! Rape! Rape!"

UPSTAIRS CORRIDOR.

Another guest at the inn, Mr. MacLachlan, stumbles out of his room, as Susan bustles past.

MAC LACHLAN: What is it, lassie?

SUSAN: There's a rape going on down there.

MAC LACHLAN: Rape!

MRS. WATERS' BEDROOM.

Tom and Fitzpatrick are still struggling. Suddenly Tom sends Fitzpatrick staggering into MacLachlan.

MAC LACHLAN: Mr. Fitzpatrick—what's this now!

FITZPATRICK: Mr. MacLachlan, dear friend—I am rejoiced to see you here. This villain has debauched my wife.

MAC LACHLAN: Your wife? What wife? Do I not know Mrs. Fitzpatrick very well? And can I not see that the lady in bed with this gentleman is not your wife at all, sir.

Fitzpatrick looks in astonishment at Mrs. Waters who peers above the sheets.

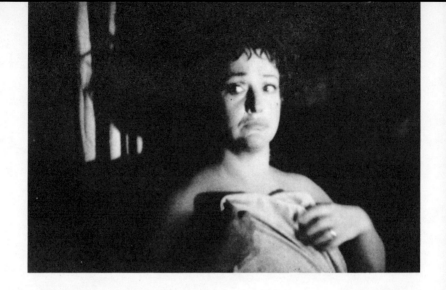

INNER COURTYARD.

SUSAN: Rape! Rape! Rape! Rape!

Susan dashes down the stairs, camera panning. Sophie and Mrs. Fitzpatrick duck underneath the stairs, horrified. The Landlady appears from another doorway and rushes, roaring, to Susan (Sophie and Mrs. Fitzpatrick are in the background of shot).

LANDLADY: Bless me, girl, what's this hullabaloo?

SUSAN: 'Tis Tom Jones, madam. In bed with Mrs. Waters and discovered by her husband.

Landlady rushes upstairs.

SUSAN: An Irish gentleman, madam.

Zoom in to close-up of Sophie.

SOPHIE (*appearing from under the stairs*): Forgive me—did you say Tom Jones?

SUSAN: Yes, madam—in bed with that trull—Mrs. Waters.

SOPHIE: Betrayed.

Sophie faints.

CORRIDOR.

Susan and the Landlady dashing down the corridor.

MRS. WATERS' BEDROOM.

The Landlady bursts in.

FITZPATRICK: Ma'am, pray forgive my dastardly intrusion. I—

LANDLADY: What in the devil's name is this disturbance?

MRS. WATERS: I thought myself in a respectable inn, but I see it's a bawdy house.

FITZPATRICK: I have made a mistake. I was looking for my wife.

MRS. WATERS: This set of villains broke into my room—

FITZPATRICK: I heartily ask your pardon, ma'am. I thought you was me wife. Although (*glares at Tom*), I see no reason for a Christian gentleman to be in a lady's bed in his shirt.

TOM: I heard the lady's screams and ran to her assistance (*he points*) from the adjoining chamber!

FITZPATRICK: Adjoining chamber!

TOM (*to Landlady*): It seems, madam, I have had the good fortune to prevent the lady being robbed.

LANDLADY: Robbed!

FITZPATRICK: Robbed! I shall have your blood for that, sir!

He lunges at Tom, who ducks. Uproar. Mrs. Waters screams "Rape!" again.

INNER COURTYARD.

Mrs. Fitzpatrick is reviving Sophie.

MRS. FITZPATRICK: Come, Sophie, we must fly before Fitzpatrick discovers me.

Sophie gets to her feet and bursts into tears.

MRS. FITZPATRICK: Oh come! Pull yourself together, child. We've got a long ride ahead of us.

Sophie rises to the occasion. Her muff is left, forgotten, on the ground. They rush out.

MRS. WATERS' BEDROOM.

Tom shakes off Fitzpatrick, kisses Mrs. Waters and exits. (This and much of the rest of this sequence is in fast motion.)

UPPER CORRIDOR.

Tom, running top speed, pauses a split second, looking at the camera. He yells, unheard, "Rape!" and dashes on.

OUTER COURTYARD.

Western and Supple hurtle in on their horses. Sophie and Mrs. Fitzpatrick duck into the shadows. Miss Western's coach follows. We pan with them as they dismount. Sophie and Mrs. Fitzpatrick slip out.

INNER COURTYARD.

Tom rushes down the stairs clad only in his shirt, camera panning. He sees Sophie's muff on the ground and immediately seizes it. Out drops her pocketbook, which he examines.

TOM: Sophie!

He thrusts the pocketbook back into the muff, with which he strokes his face lovingly. He dashes on, running into Western who has just entered by the archway. Western yells and flies at Tom's throat.

WESTERN: I got you, you fox. Well, the vixen can't be far away.

Tom struggles loose and doubles back up the stairs into Fitzpatrick's arms. He ducks. All give chase. Uproar.

MRS. WATERS' BEDROOM.

Tom dashes to the bed, grabs his trousers and says farewell to Mrs. Waters.

TOM: Good-bye, madam, I regret I must take my leave of you.

Mrs. Waters waves farewell. Tom jumps through the window as the rest follow. Pan from one door to the other as Fitzpatrick, Western, MacLachlan, Supple, Susan, etc., arrive in full cry. Seeing them, Mrs. Waters cries, "Rape! Rape!"

WESTERN: Ods Zodikins!

124

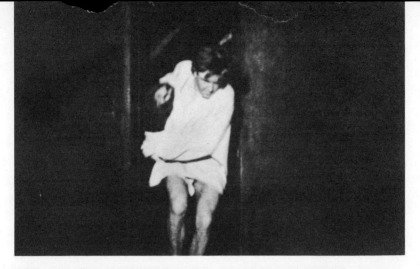

All give chase except Fitzgerald. He gives Mrs. Waters a look. She shrugs.

OUTER COURTYARD.

Tom, still in his shirt, drops into the courtyard. He dashes to the carriage standing there in order to change. A horrified Miss Western discovers him.

MISS WESTERN: Oh! the villain! Brother! Brother!

TOM: Miss Western!

Tom escapes into the night. Gunshots are fired. A bell rings.

Western, Miss Western, Supple, Landlord, Landlady, MacLachlan, Susan rush in cursing and swearing after Tom. General chaos and confusion.

MRS. WATERS' BEDROOM.

Mr. Fitzpatrick prepares to get into bed with Mrs. Waters. As he takes off his belt, she is kicking her heels up and down in anticipation. He pinches out the candle. The din continues.

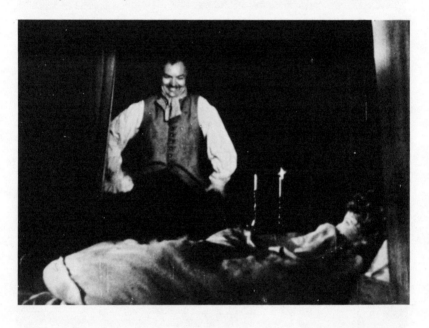

CROSSROADS. ROAD TO LONDON. DAY.

Western and Parson Supple approaching on horses, Miss Western's coach behind.

SUPPLE: Don't be dismayed sir. She will soon be tired with her journey and stop in some inn. She's bound for London, I'm sure.

WESTERN: Paugh! Damn the girl!

He sniffs the air keenly. The sound of a hunt in chase gets louder.

WESTERN: I am lamenting the loss of such a fine morning for hunting. It is confounded hard to lose one of the finest scenting days of the season.

MOORS.

Western's eyeline: a hunt flashes past in the valley below. The Squire roars and his horse starts.

WESTERN: Ah, whoa. Come on.

Western pretends his horse is out of control. He claps his heels into his horse and is off after the hunt. Supple hesitates, then follows, camera panning. Miss Western is left leaning out of her coach shouting.

MISS WESTERN: Brother! What are you doing? Dobson, drive on.

A masked Footpad (Partridge) appears and points his pistol.

FOOTPAD: Stand and deliver.

The coachman, clearly afraid, puts his hands above his head. Miss Western, completely assured, pokes her head out of the window and addresses the Footpad, while indicating the pistol.

MISS WESTERN (*glaring*): What—did you say, sir?

FOOTPAD: Stand and deliver!

MISS WESTERN: Deliver! I am no wandering midwife, sir. Deliver what?

FOOTPAD: Stand—

MISS WESTERN: I will not stand for you sir, no, nor for any man!

FOOTPAD (*desperate*): Madam—

MISS WESTERN: Don't you point that firearm at me, sir!

The Footpad, taken aback, hesitates, but before he has time to make up his mind, Miss Western addresses the coachman.

MISS WESTERN: Dobson, drive on.

The coach goes on, leaving the Footpad almost in tears.

ANOTHER PART OF THE MOOR.

Tom is walking along a country road. He has Sophie's muff.

COMMENTATOR: It is hard when a woman leaves a man nothing but memories and a muff.

Tom turns a corner and camera zooms back to reveal a pistol in corner of frame. It is the Footpad. At pistol point, he makes his demand.

FOOTPAD: Your money or your life!

TOM: I only have one guinea, sir.

PARTRIDGE: Give it here.

Tom flips the coin and catches hold of the Footpad's hand, turning the muzzle from him. The Footpad crashes from his pathetic nag. In a flash Tom has the man flat on the ground.

TOM (*amused*): I'm afraid as a "gentleman of the road" you've cut a very poor figure.

FOOTPAD: Be merciful, sir. I didn't mean any harm. Truly, I didn't.

TOM (*holding pistol*): No harm?

FOOTPAD: It isn't loaded.

Tom examines the revolver.

TOM: Nor is it!

FOOTPAD: I'm not a bandit by profession, sir. Just a poor man down on his luck. Mine, sir, is a sad story.

Tom is inclined to believe him, the Footpad looks so pathetic.

Tom is now on the horse, the Footpad walking along beside it.

FOOTPAD: The start of my ruin was twenty years ago. It was all over one Tom Jones.

TOM: What do you mean?

FOOTPAD: At that time I was employed as a barber by a Mr. Allworthy. One day he found a baby abandoned in his bed. I was accused of being the father.

TOM: Then your name is—

PARTRIDGE: Partridge.

TOM: Father!

Tom pulls Partridge up and throws himself effusively on his neck.

Partridge is now riding on the horse, and Tom is leading it.

PARTRIDGE: But I do assure you, sir, that there was no truth in the accusation.

TOM: Then who was my father?

PARTRIDGE: None of us ever discovered. That was the whole beginning of my downfall.

TOM: Mr. Partridge, how can I make up for the suffering you have had on my account?

PARTRIDGE: Would you take me on as your servant, sir?

TOM (*shaking his hand*): My companion in misfortune!

PARTRIDGE: Oh sir.

Both Tom and Partridge are now walking beside the horse as they pass a signpost marked "To London."

TOM (*reflectively*): Are lodgings cheap to come by in London? I have no money.

PARTRIDGE: I know an old lady who runs a lodging house in London. She was Mr. Allworthy's cook when I was his barber. We will go there.

TOM: No friend of Mr. Allworthy's will speak to me now.

PARTRIDGE: But Mrs. Miller is one of the kindest ladies I know. Who knows? She may yet get you back in his favor.

LONDON

A LONDON STREET. DAY.

TECHNICAL NOTE

(*At this point, the film changes style somewhat. Till now we have been in the subdued and natural atmosphere of the countryside in which Tom has grown up and to which he is used. Every day he has seen the colors and sobriety—the greens, the browns, the*

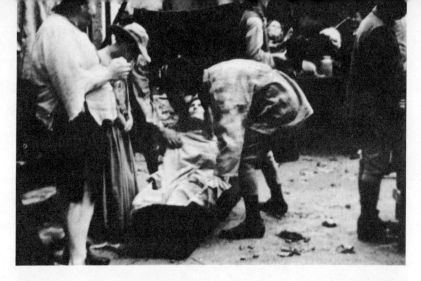

stones—*of the landscape reflected in itself; now he sees a world of luxury and vice heightened as it must be in the eyes of a country boy. The color of the film takes on a new violence and garishness. The characters a viciousness in the world of a Rake's Progress and Gin Lane.*)

Camera tracks down a squalid street. Every sign of violence, drunkenness, misery, debauchery. A prostitute offers her services.

PROSTITUTE: You're a lovely boy. Won't you come with a lady?

TOM: No. No thank you.

Tom shrugs off other propositions.

ANOTHER LONDON STREET.

A contrasting London street. Well-dressed people moving about.

EXTERIOR: MRS. FITZPATRICK'S LODGINGS.

Tom is at the door.

MRS. FITZPATRICK'S DRAWING ROOM.

COMMENTATOR: Desperate to find his Sophie, Tom called on Mrs. Fitzpatrick, who was entertaining a certain Lady Bellaston, the notorious Lady Bellaston.

Abigail enters.

ABIGAIL: It's the handsome young gentleman again, madam, inquiring for Miss Western.

Mrs. Fitzpatrick and Lady Bellaston are sipping chocolate. Lady Bellaston is a beautiful, vivacious lady; clever, dominant, somewhat vindictive.

MRS. FITZPATRICK: You see, Bella, how persistent he is. His servant discovered this address and ever since he persecutes us. Send him away, Abigail. Tell him Miss Western is no longer here.

ABIGAIL: Yes, ma'am.

Abigail bobs and goes out. Lady Bellaston crosses to window.

MRS. FITZPATRICK: Bella, you must let Sophie come and stay with you. My protector is coming back and I fear he might take too much interest in my cousin.

LADY BELLASTON: Oh, Harriet, you can always rely upon me.

STREET.

Lady Bellaston's eyeline of Tom saying good-bye to Abigail, and crossing the street. He is carrying Sophie's muff.

EXTERIOR: MRS. FITZPATRICK'S LODGINGS.

Close shot Lady Bellaston at window. She is fascinated.

MRS. FITZPATRICK'S DRAWING ROOM.

Lady Bellaston turns back from the window.

LADY BELLASTON: Your little maid is obviously in the right. He is a very pretty fellow. No wonder so many women are fond of him.

Mrs. Fitzpatrick has gone to the window to look too. Lady Bellaston, her eyes dilating lecherously, returns to the chocolate.

LADY BELLASTON: Harriet, we must do what we can for Sophie. The girl is obviously intoxicated and nothing less than ruin will content her.

She smiles and drinks her chocolate.

MRS. MILLER'S DRAWING ROOM. DAY.

Tom sits musing by the fireplace.

TOM (*somewhat distracted*): I'm absolutely certain Sophie was at Mrs. Fitzpatrick's when I called.

Mrs. Miller, a kindly white-haired lady of about sixty, sits sewing. She has taken a great liking to Tom despite the situation with Allworthy who supports her.

TOM: Dear Mrs. Miller, what am I to do? No friends. No money. No introductions. And I know nothing of London.

MRS. MILLER: You're not to worry about the money, Mr. Jones. You can stay here for the moment.

TOM: You're very kind, Mrs. Miller.

Partridge suddenly bursts in with a package.

PARTRIDGE: For you, Tom. It's just arrived. I wonder what it can be.

MRS. MILLER: What is it?

Partridge unwraps the bundle. The bundle opens to reveal a domino, a mask, an invitation to a masquerade.

TOM: It's an invitation to a masked ball. (*Reads:*) "The Queen of the fairies sends you this: Treat her favors not amiss." Mrs. Fitzpatrick perhaps with news of my Sophie!

MRS. MILLER: Or Miss Sophie herself.

Tom puts on the domino and mask. He smiles.

A GARDEN. NIGHT.

COMMENTATOR: Vauxhall Gardens, where people come to see and to be seen. In heaps they run, some to undo and some to be undone.

Long shot. This is the most spectacular color sequence in the film. Red, oranges, purples, crowd the luxury and brilliance of Vauxhall and Ranelagh. Lanterns glow in the trees. The masquerade is in progress and Tom and Partridge are looking around.

Partridge grabs a likely girl and disappears. Tom questions every woman in sight.

ANOTHER PART OF THE GARDEN.

Miss Western and the Squire, heavily and ludicrously disguised.

WESTERN: It's no fun for a man like me to be dolled up in this damned flummery.

MISS WESTERN: All folks of fashion are here. Sophie will be no exception.

WESTERN: Well, show her to me and I'll have her arrested.

MISS WESTERN: Arrested! Do you imagine a woman of stature can be arrested in a civilized nation?

WESTERN: A pretty civilized nation, indeed, where women are above the law. Civilized nation, my trunk.

MISS WESTERN: Je vous mesprise de tout mon coeur! Now where can my niece be?

ANOTHER PART OF THE GARDEN.

Tom gets small change from many of the women but finds he is doing quite nicely with a girl dressed as a shepherdess, when

a wand taps his shoulder. Tom turns.

Big close-up of Lady Bellaston dressed as the Queen of the Fairies in an elaborate costume and mask.

LADY BELLASTON: If you engage any longer with that trollop, I shall tell Miss Western.

Lady Bellaston nods and walks away.

Tom, thinking it is Mrs. Fitzpatrick, follows her through the bizarre jostling figures as a dance is in progress, camera tracking. He loses her figure and is about to give up the search when he sees her in an arbor near the dancers. She beckons and the camera pans him over to her.

TOM: Is Sophie here then, madam?

LADY BELLASTON: Upon my honor, Miss Western is not here.

They move into the throng and start to dance.

TOM: Indeed, Mrs. Fitzpatrick—if you are she—it is a little cruel of you to divert yourself at my expense.

LADY BELLASTON: And do you imagine, good sir, that I have no better regard for my cousin than to assist her in carrying on an affair between you two, which must end in her ruin?

TOM: Madam, that is the last thing I would wish.

LADY BELLASTON: If the Queen of the Fairies had so little regard for you and Sophie, she would not have appointed to meet you here.

Tom's eyeline, panning of Lady Bellaston weaving through the dance. Lady Bellaston's eyeline of her prey; panning. Two shots as Tom and Lady Bellaston come together in the dance.

LADY BELLASTON: Confess honestly. Are you used, Mr. Jones, to make these sudden conquests?

TOM: I am used, madam, to submit. If you take my heart by surprise, the rest of my body has the right to follow.

Lady Bellaston prepares to leave.

LADY BELLASTON: I hope you won't follow me. I protest I shall not know what to say if you do.

Lady Bellaston taps Tom on the lips with her wand, and leaves.

Tom follows.

Lady Bellaston gets into a sedan chair. Not having the price of a fare himself, Tom cheerfully follows behind her on foot, jeered at by the unhired chairmen. Lawyer Dowling appears, watching Tom. He hails a sedan chair.

LADY BELLASTON'S HOUSE. STAIRS. NIGHT.

Camera looks down into the hall. Lady Bellaston comes up toward camera and mounts the staircase. Tom pauses, examining a life-size statue of a male nude in the hall. He follows her up the stairs.

LADY BELLASTON'S BEDROOM.

Tom closes the door behind him. Tom stands transfixed as camera pans and tracks to close shot of Lady Bellaston. She unmasks.

TOM: I thought you were Mrs. Fitzpatrick.

LADY BELLASTON: Fitzpatrick!

She laughs provocatively and then, so does he.

LADY BELLASTON: Sir, I am unfamiliar with customs in the country, but in town it is considered impolite to keep a lady waiting. (*She seats herself at the foot of the bed.*)

Tom looks at the camera, then he advances. He joins Lady Bellaston on the bed. They embrace. The image freezes.

COMMENTATOR: With our usual good breeding we will not follow this particular conversation further, but attend results on the following day.

INTERIOR. TAILOR'S SHOP. DAY.

COMMENTATOR: Our hero released from Lady Bellaston a torrent of affection as well as a flood of gifts, which he found suitably embarrassing and quite irresistible.

Tom is examining various garments, watched approvingly by Lady Bellaston who is obviously footing the bill. Tailors and assistants hover around measuring, fitting, presenting articles of various kinds. After running her finger appreciatively over Tom's cheek, Lady Bellaston prepares to go.

LADY BELLASTON: We must have you looking your best.

TOM: Lady Bellaston—

LADY BELLASTON: Isn't that what Miss Western would want? Come back precisely at four. I shall have news for you then.

She turns to the shopkeeper.

LADY BELLASTON: Send the bill to me, sir.

TAILOR: Yes, my lady. Very good, my lady. Good day, my lady.

She goes out.

LADY BELLASTON'S ENTRANCE. DAY.

An elegant door knocker is rapped. The door is opened by a

Negro boy. Camera tilts up to Tom, looking very handsome in- deed in his new finery, with a cane in his hand. The Negro boy gasps with admiration and steps back, admitting Tom.

HALL AND STAIRS.

Tom strides across the hall and starts up the stairs.

DRAWING ROOM.

Tom sails grandly into the drawing room, thinking he will find Lady Bellaston. He admires himself in the mirror and practices bowing.

COMMENTATOR: How could Tom know that Sophie was now staying here with Lady Bellaston, and being besieged by a certain Lord Fellamar, a gentleman with an eye for any beauty, especially when a fortune was attached.

HALL AND STAIRS.

Boy opens front door, admitting Sophie, followed by Lord Fella-

141

mar. She has left the play early. Lady Bellaston is late.

FELLAMAR: I do beg to excuse the play, but when may I see you again?

SOPHIE: Forgive me, my lord, but I am afraid my plans for remaining in London are still a little uncertain. Good day, my lord.

Sophie moves toward the stairs.

DRAWING ROOM.

Tom at the mirror, trying snuff. He sneezes as Sophie enters. Close-up: Tom.

TOM: Sophie . . .

Close-up: Sophie.

SOPHIE: Tom!

TOM: I see, Sophie you're somewhat surprised—

SOPHIE: What are you doing here?

TOM: I came to look for you. (*Sneezes.*)

She assumes a reserved air, moving away from him.

TOM: I found your pocketbook at Upton, and came to ask if I might return it.

SOPHIE: How dare you mention that place to me?

TOM: Oh, my Sophie, let me ask your pardon!

SOPHIE: My pardon! After what I heard at the inn!

Tom reels under her disdain.

TOM: You cannot despise me more than I do myself.

She looks mollified and softens suddenly. There is a noise and they turn. Tom and Sophie's eyeline as Lady Bellaston enters. Her face at first is all eagerness, is immediately forged into the look of a wicked meat-axe. Sophie is very disconcerted.

LADY BELLASTON: I thought, Miss Western, you were at the play.

SOPHIE: The play caused so violent an uproar that I got frightened and came home, where I found this gentleman. He has apparently found the pocketbook I told your Ladyship I lost and wishes to return it.

Tom stands looking thoroughly foolish while Lady Bellaston looks suspicious and displeased. Tom makes a desperate effort to recover his composure.

TOM: And when I do bring it, all that I ask is that I might have the honor of presenting it in person.

Close-up: Lady Bellaston.

LADY BELLASTON (*between her teeth*): I presume, sir, you are a gentleman and my doors are never shut to people of fashion.

TOM: Thank you, madam. Ladies. (*He starts to leave.*)

LADY BELLASTON: Your cane, sir.

Tom attempts a graceful exit. Another sneeze destroys it. Two pairs of hungry eyes follow him. Lady Bellaston then looks icily at Sophie. Lady Bellaston seats herself at her writing desk.

LADY BELLASTON: A handsome fellow. I don't remember ever to have seen his face before.

SOPHIE: Nor I neither, madam.

LADY BELLASTON: I suspected it was Mr. Jones himself.

SOPHIE (*blushing and affecting a laugh*): Did your ladyship, indeed?

LADY BELLASTON: Yes. I can't imagine what put the idea into my head for, to give this fellow his due, he was very well dressed. I think, dear Sophie, that is not often the case with your friend.

SOPHIE: I thought your Ladyship had said he was handsome.

LADY BELLASTON: Whom, pray?

Close-up.

SOPHIE: Mr. Jones.

Close-up of Lady Bellaston reacting.

SOPHIE (*she recollects herself*): I meant, of course, the gentleman that was with us just now.

LADY BELLASTON: Sophie! Oh Sophie! This Mr. Jones, I fear, still runs in your head.

SOPHIE: I assure you, madam, Mr. Jones means no more to me than the gentleman who just left us.

144

Lady Bellaston kisses Sophie.

LADY BELLASTON: Forgive me teasing you. I promise I'll never mention his name again.

Lady Bellaston reflects for a moment, and rings a bell. Sophie leaves. The Negro boy enters.

LADY BELLASTON: Take this to Lord Fellamar and beg him to attend me tomorrow.

LADY BELLASTON'S BEDROOM. DAY.

Lady Bellaston is at her dressing table, dressed in négligée and making up. Lord Fellamar is sitting beside her eagerly listening.

LADY BELLASTON: She is the only daughter of a country booby squire.

LORD FELLAMAR: At the playhouse she blazed like a star. The first moment I saw her I loved her to distraction.

LADY BELLASTON: Her father's estate is a good £3,000 a year.

Lord Fellamar takes this in.

LORD FELLAMAR: Then madam, I think her the best match in England.

LADY BELLASTON: Then if you like her, my lord, you shall have her.

MRS. MILLER'S LODGINGS. TOM'S BEDROOM. DAY.

Tom, in shirt sleeves and breeches, opens his door to Honor.

TOM: Honor!

HONOR: A letter from my mistress, Mr. Jones.

Tom reacts to a voice from downstairs and pulls Honor into the bedroom, closing the door. He pushes Honor behind the curtains of the bed, and puts the letter under a pillow on the bed. He is only just in time to conceal them from Lady Bellaston who enters. Lady Bellaston is obviously in the mood to dally.

TOM: My dear charming Lady Bellaston.

LADY BELLASTON: Dear! Charming! You have been avoiding me. I should scold you. But I don't think I intend to.

Lady Bellaston confidently closes the door behind her.

TOM: Sh! There is a lady—

LADY BELLASTON: A lady? One of your ladies, I suppose? Where is she?

She starts looking. Tom grabs her.

146

TOM: I—I—There is a lady in the next room. A-dying, madam.

LADY BELLASTON: What scheme have you and Sophie been plotting behind my back?

TOM: Madam, I don't understand.

LADY BELLASTON: Answer me one question only: have you not betrayed my honor to her?

Tom takes her in his arms. Honor peers through the curtains.

LADY BELLASTON: Am I neglected, slighted for a country girl, for an idiot!

TOM: Neglected, madam?

LADY BELLASTON: Oh!!

They kiss. Honor peeks again, irrepressibly curious, but shocked.

Tom signals for her to leave. Tom manages to keep Lady Bellaston occupied with the kiss as Honor leaves, outraged.

Lady Bellaston lies half asleep, though still half-way to the boil. Tom is making intricate efforts to read Sophie's letter behind

147

Lady Bellaston's head. When she tries to turn her head Tom holds it in passionate coventry below his armpit which makes the Lady purr.

COMMENTATOR: "I charge you not to think of visiting again," Sophie desperately wrote to Tom. "The truth would certainly be discovered . . . something favorable perhaps may happen, until then we must be patient."

Tom looks a little disappointed, slips the letter beneath the pillow, kissing it as he does so. Lady Bellaston manages to wrench her head free, being just about to come to the boil.

LADY BELLASTON'S DRAWING ROOM. NIGHT.

It is after supper and Lady Bellaston and Lord Fellamar, Sophie and a Mr. Edwards, an old flame of Lady Bellaston's, are playing whist. They are intent on the game. Camera pans down under the table. Lord Fellamar's leg rubs against Sophie. She moves her leg away and the game continues.

Lord Fellamar's hand strays on to Sophie's knee. She gives him a sharp rap.

Lord Fellamar smiles.

Sophie tries to ignore him.

Behind her cards Lady Bellaston slyly winks at Lord Fellamar. The game continues.

LADY BELLASTON (*softly*): Courage, mon vieux.

LADY BELLASTON'S BEDROOM. DAY.

Next morning, Lady Bellaston is having her morning chocolate. Sophie is with her, sitting on the bed dressed. Lady Bellaston is looking more than ever like a happy, sleek, plotting pussy.

LADY BELLASTON: Lord Fellamar is one of the most gallant young fellows about town. You would be mad to refuse him.

SOPHIE: Then I shall most certainly be mad.

There is a knock at the door.

LADY BELLASTON: Entrez.

The door opens to reveal Lord Fellamar.

Sophie rises, curtsies to Lord Fellamar and goes out.

Dejectedly Lord Fellamar crosses to Lady Bellaston, kisses her hand and sits on the bed.

LORD FELLAMAR: Madam, Miss Western is hardly encouraging.

LADY BELLASTON: My dear lord, you certainly need a cordial. Fie upon it, have more resolution. Are you frightened by the word rape?

Lord Fellamar is indeed.

LADY BELLASTON: All woman love a man of spirit. Remember the story of the Sabine ladies. I believe they made tolerably good wives afterwards. Come this evening at nine. I will see she is alone.

Lord Fellamar nods excitedly. Lady Bellaston smiles.

LONDON STREET. DAY.

Camera tracks along a street down which Tom and Partridge are strolling. Horses and carriage pass beside them.

TOM: Oh my dear friend, I am so entangled with this woman I don't know how to extricate myself.

Partridge thinks for a moment. He stops.

PARTRIDGE: I know, propose marriage to her.

TOM (*horror struck*): To Lady Bellaston?

PARTRIDGE: Ay, propose marriage to her and she will call off in a moment. You've not a penny, and she'll think you are marrying her for her wealth. It's very convincing for a man in your desperate situation.

They start walking again. Camera continues tracking.

TOM: But what if she takes me at my word. Then I'm caught in my own trap.

PARTRIDGE: I promise you she won't. She'll be the one to break it off.

They pass out of shot.

That evening the curtains are drawn and the candles lit. Sophie is weeping over a novel. There is a noise and she rises as Lord Fellamar bursts into the room.

SOPHIE: Lord Fellamar!

LORD FELLAMAR: Yes, Miss Western, it is I. I fear I break in upon you abruptly.

SOPHIE: Indeed my lord, I am a little surprised.

LORD FELLAMAR: Love—love has deprived me of all reason.

He comes toward her, kneels at her feet, and thrusts a bouquet at her. Sophie edges behind the sofa.

SOPHIE: My lord, I neither understand your words nor your behavior.

Lord Fellamar moves in for the kill.

LORD FELLAMAR: Oh, you're the most adorable, most divine creature.

SOPHIE: I do assure you, my lord, I shall not want to hear any more of this.

Sophie goes to the door, but Lord Fellamar is there first.

LORD FELLAMAR: If I were master of the world, I would lay it at your feet.

SOPHIE: My lord, I beg you to stop.

Lord Fellamar grabs her hand.

SOPHIE (*continues*): Let go my hand. I will never see you again.

LORD FELLAMAR: Then madam, I must make the best use of this moment.

SOPHIE (*preparing to scream*): What do you mean?

LORD FELLAMAR: I have no fear but of losing you, madam.

She screams. A chase ensues and Sophie slips and falls to the floor. Lord Fellamar pounces upon her. Camera pans with Sophie and looks down on her as they grapple.

HALL.

The page opens the front door and in bursts Squire Western followed by Mr. Supple. Western reacts to Sophie's screaming.

WESTERN: Where is she? Damn me if I won't unkennel her now!

DRAWING ROOM.

Lord Fellamar hears the noise and quickly scrambles to his feet.

Sophie does the same. The door flies open and Western comes in hooting triumphantly.

SOPHIE: Oh, Father!

LORD FELLAMAR (*more embarrassed than ever*): Your father?

WESTERN: Yes, and who in hell are you?

Lord Fellamar is straightening his wig.

LORD FELLAMAR: I sir, am Lord Fellamar and I am the happy man whom I hope you will accept as your son-in-law.

WESTERN: You are a son-of-a-whore for all your fancy fol-de-rols.

LORD FELLAMAR: I resent your tone, sir.

WESTERN: Resent me arse. I'll teach you to father-in-law me.

He grabs the half-naked Sophie and hoists her up on his shoulders like a sack of corn. Then he dashes past the astonished Supple, hooting and hallooing.

SOPHIE: Oh father, put me down.

Lord Fellamar looks after them, dazed.

LADY BELLASTON'S BEDROOM. DAY.

Lady Bellaston is having her wig dressed by her maid as she reads a letter from Tom.

COMMENTATOR: "Dearest Madam," Tom had carefully written, "I am extremely concerned for fear your reputation should be exposed. There is only one way to secure it, that you bestow on me the legal right to call you mine forever. Thomas Jones."

Lady Bellaston looks irritated, then furious, then trapped. She crumples the letter and turns to her maid, saying furiously:

LADY BELLASTON: Understand this . . . I shall not receive Mr. Jones if he calls here again.

The maid turns, looks straight into camera and gives a slow wink.

154

LADY BELLASTON'S DRAWING ROOM. DAY.

Miss Western and Lady Bellaston are taking tea.

COMMENTATOR: In London love and scandal are considered the best sweeteners of tea.

MISS WESTERN: I do not doubt that my niece will welcome the favors of a gentleman like Lord Fellamar. This Blifil is a hideous kind of fellow. But as you know, Belle, all country gentlemen are.

LADY BELLASTON: I don't then wonder at Sophie's infatuation for this Jones creature. He's an agreeable fellow to look at. Miss Western, will you believe me when I tell you that he has had the audacity to make love to me?

An expression of indignation from Miss Western.

MISS WESTERN: Oh, these men! I would have torn the eyes out of a prince if he had attempted such freedoms with me.

Lady Bellaston smiles.

LADY BELLASTON: Indeed he has even gone so far as to propose marriage to me.

She takes out Tom's letter and shows it to Miss Western.

MISS WESTERN: With your leave, Belle, I will show this to my niece.

LADY BELLASTON: Apply it to what purpose you may please.

MRS. MILLER'S. TOM'S BEDROOM. DAY.

Tom, handed a letter by Partridge, is excitedly pleased to recognize by the writing that it is from Sophie. He opens and reads it.

TOM: It's from my Sophie.

PARTRIDGE: Good.

COMMENTATOR: "Sir," she wrote, "my Aunt has just now shown me a letter from you to Lady Bellaston which contains a proposal of marriage. All I desire is that your name may never more be mentioned to your obliged humble servant. Sophie Western."

Tom and Partridge exchange miserable glances. Then Partridge makes a hopeful suggestion.

PARTRIDGE: You could try Mrs. Fitzpatrick. She might be able to help.

Tom pulls off his wig, disconsolate.

EXTERIOR. MRS. MILLER'S LODGINGS.

COMMENTATOR: 'Tis said that hope is a bad supper but makes a good breakfast, and in the morning Tom set off for Mrs. Fitzpatrick to seek help. Not a moment too soon, for who should arrive but his old benefactor Squire Allworthy.

Tom comes and turns down the street. A coach pulls up at the house. Allworthy gets out to be greeted by an enraptured Mrs. Miller.

MRS. MILLER: Mr. Allworthy! What an unexpected pleasure!

ALLWORTHY: Good morning, Mrs. Miller.

MRS. MILLER: You have come to forgive him.

ALLWORTHY: Forgive whom, Mrs. Miller?

MRS. MILLER: Dear Mr. Jones.

Blifil alights from the coach.

ALLWORTHY: Mr. Jones here, madam? No, I've come to bring my nephew, Mr. Blifil, to London.

EXTERIOR. MRS. FITZPATRICK'S LODGINGS.

Tom comes down the street followed by two thugs. Camera pans his turn to Fitzpatrick's door. Tom knocks. The two thugs dodge

out of sight down an intersecting street. The door of Mrs. Fitzpatrick's lodging is opened to admit Tom.

MRS. FITZPATRICK'S DRAWING ROOM.

MRS. FITZPATRICK: She must be the most contemptible of women who can overlook merit such as yours.

Tom realizes what is coming and reacts to camera.

EXTERIOR. MRS. FITZPATRICK'S LODGINGS.

COMMENTATOR: An old acquaintance arrives.

Down the other intersecting street, the worse for drink, comes Mr. Fitzpatrick, telling the world at large that he is after finding his disreputable wife.

FITZPATRICK: . . . where the dirty whore's living now. You wait till I get my hands on' her! I'll break every bone in her body!

While tottering along, he bumps into the two thugs in their hiding place. He shoves them out of his way.

DRAWING ROOM.

It is clear by this time Mrs. Fitzpatrick is mixing business with pleasure. She is trying to captivate an embarrassed Tom. Tom gets up to go.

MRS. FITZPATRICK: Let us meet tomorrow. We will find a way of easing your predicament.

TOM: Er . . . Yes, tomorrow.

She looks at him winningly as he goes out.

TOM: Thank you.

EXTERIOR. MRS. FITZPATRICK'S LODGINGS.

Mr. Fitzpatrick arrives at the door of the house as Tom is coming out of it. They bump into each other.

TOM: I'm very sorry. (*Recognizing Fitzpatrick.*) My dear sir, I hope there is no ill blood remaining between us.

MR. FITZPATRICK: Upon my soul, sir, I don't remember your name.

TOM: Nor I yours, but I remember your face from the inn at Upton.

MR. FITZPATRICK: Upton! Then your name is Tom Jones?

TOM: Indeed it is, sir.

MR. FITZPATRICK: Then you have been with my wife after all. (*He strikes him a blow.*) Well, there's that for you, you rascal. And if you don't give me satisfaction for that blow I'll give you another. Come on, fight, damn you.

Fitzpatrick then draws his sword. Tom, dazed, does the same, and they fence their way down the street. A crowd draws around.

The fight is to be shot close, in quick panning shots. There are screams and shrieks from the crowd as a cart is overturned, a horse bolts, scaffolding is overturned. Fitzpatrick is badly wounded.

161

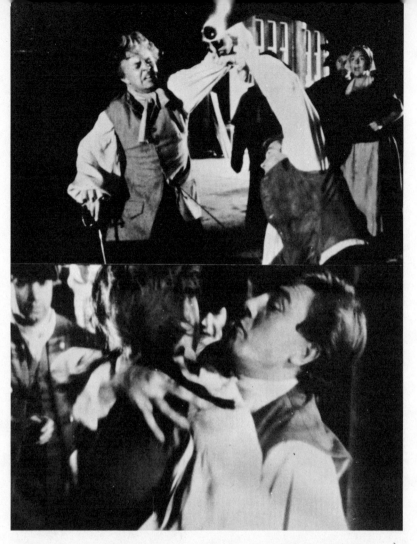

TOM (*gets up*): I'm sorry, sir, but you drew this on yourself.

At this moment the two thugs come out of hiding and seize Tom roughly.

FIRST THUG (*yelling*): You're a liar. You set on that gentleman to rob him.

The crowd turns on Tom. Cries of "Thief," "Murderer," etc. The Watch arrive. Tom starts to protest, but the crowd roars him down.

LONDON STREET.

Blifil and Dowling are deep in conversation. They are watched from a doorway by the two thugs.

DOWLING: Yes, for armed robbery.

BLIFIL: And you're certain the bastard will be hanged?

DOWLING: No doubt about it. (*Indicating thugs.*) I hired these two to follow Master Jones, which they did with rare zeal.

BLIFIL: Good. See that they are properly taken care of, will you?

(*He hands Dowling the money.*) I will break the news to my uncle.

Blifil and Dowling part company. Dowling goes toward the thugs, who come forward to meet him.

MRS. MILLER'S DRAWING ROOM. DAY.

Allworthy and Mrs. Miller are having tea together.

MRS. MILLER: Mr. Jones has one of the kindest hearts I know. He never mentions your name but to praise it.

Blifil opens the door. He is at his most sanctimonious.

BLIFIL: Uncle, I am afraid to tell you what has happened. It may shock you too much.

ALLWORTHY: What's the matter, nephew?

BLIFIL: Your adopted son, sir, Jones, has proved himself one of the greatest villains on earth.

Mrs. Miller rises indignantly.

MRS. MILLER: If anyone else had called him a villain, I would have thrown this boiling tea in his face.

ALLWORTHY: Mrs. Miller!

MRS. MILLER: I know he's not without faults—but they are those of wildness and youth—(*She looks pointedly at Blifil.*) And I'm sure many of us have worse.

Allworthy is about to defend Blifil.

BLIFIL: At least we are not footpads, Mrs. Miller.

MRS. MILLER: What do you mean?

BLIFIL: Mr. Jones has attacked a man. He has been sentenced to be hanged at Tyburn. Nobody can save him now!

Mrs. Miller is crying.

MONTAGE SEQUENCE. INTERIOR. NEWGATE JAIL.

Various shots of prisoners.

STREET SINGER (*off screen*):

> If he swing by the string,
> He will hear the bells ring,
> And then there's an end to Tommy.

> He must hang by the noose,
> And no hand'll cut loose
> The noose from the neck of poor Tommy.

> If he swing . . .
> If he swing . . .

Camera tracking with Tom behind bars.

COMMENTATOR: And Tom was to swing, his enemies had determined on that.

FITZPATRICK'S LODGINGS. BEDROOM. DAY.

COMMENTATOR: So lawyer Dowling decided to pay a call on Mr. Fitzpatrick. And who should receive him but Mrs. Waters.

Mrs. Waters, in outdoor clothes, is putting the finishing touches to her make-up in a mirror. A knock at the door. Mrs. Waters answers it. Dowling comes in.

DOWLING: Strictly confidential. I come from a most worthy gentleman, whose name at the moment, I am not at liberty to divulge.

Mrs. Waters points to a chair.

MRS. WATERS: What does this mysterious gentleman want with me?

DOWLING: He wants you to help him see that justice is done: to make sure Jones gets his just deserts. For any assistance you can give him, he is prepared to pay handsomely.

MRS. WATERS: He is? You interest me, sir. What is the proposition?

Dowling goes on speaking, but we fade his voice down.

INTERIOR. NEWGATE JAIL. DAY.

Camera holds Tom as he paces up and down.

GIN ALLEY.

COMMENTATOR: Meanwhile faithful Partridge searched for any-

166

one who could prove Tom's innocence of the charge against him.

In a typically Hogarthian street, the camera pans and tracks with Partridge scrutinizing the faces of groups of disreputable loungers, hoping to identify the thug with the scarred cheek. Partridge sees a constable and approaches him.

PARTRIDGE: Constable, constable. Have you seen a man with a big scar on his cheek?

CONSTABLE: No, I can't say as I have. But all the rogues in the district haunt that tavern yonder.

PARTRIDGE: Will you accompany me?

CONSTABLE: I don't go searching for trouble, friend. It's easy enough to come by.

Camera pans with Partridge as he walks down the street. He comes upon the thugs who turn and stare drunkenly at him.

PARTRIDGE: Excuse me. Are you the two gentlemen who saw the fight with Mr. Jones? Tom cannot escape the gallows unless you retract your evidence. I beg you to do so. And in the meantime I assure you you will be rewarded.

FIRST THUG: Harkee' sir, everything we said was true. Now if I were you I'd be off or you are going to be the worse for it.

The first thug gives Partridge a shove, spitting after him.

FITZPATRICK'S LODGINGS. BEDROOM. DAY.

COMMENTATOR: Only one hope was left now poor Partridge, Fitzpatrick.

Fitzpatrick is lying on a bed in the foreground, groaning. Mrs. Waters is beside him, helping. She is dressed in a loose robe and her hair streams down her neck.

MRS. WATERS: Now that's better. . . .

A knock

MRS. WATERS: Come in.

Camera pans with her as she moves into the drawing room, pulling the bedroom curtains behind her. Partridge enters.

PARTRIDGE: Sorry for the intrusion, Mrs. Fitzpatrick.

MRS. WATERS: Why, if it isn't Mr. Partridge.

At this moment Partridge recognizes her as Jenny Jones of the prologue.

PARTRIDGE: Jenny Jones!

They stand regarding one another in mutual astonishment and wonder.

MRS. WATERS: But I'm Mrs. Waters now.

PARTRIDGE: Whatever are you doing here?

They sit together on a loveseat.

MRS. WATERS: I am a close friend of Mr. Fitzpatrick. I am looking after him.

PARTRIDGE: Well, indeed! I came to see Mr. Fitzpatrick to plead for your son.

MRS. WATERS: My son!

168

PARTRIDGE: Your son Tom Jones. He never intended to wound Mr. Fitzpatrick.

MRS. WATERS: But I met the man who wounded Mr. Fitzpatrick, at Upton.

PARTRIDGE: Then that is the same man, your son, Tom Jones.

Mrs. Waters looks into the camera with amazement, rather less dismayed than delighted.

Allworthy, Mrs. Miller and Partridge standing.

ALLWORTHY: With his own mother! With Jenny Jones!

PARTRIDGE: But how could either of them have known, sir?

ALLWORTHY: Good heavens, in what miserable distresses do vice and imprudence involve men.

Allworthy has moved to the mirror and pounded his fist against the mantle. The maid enters.

MAID: Ma'am, there's a Mrs. Waters here to see Mr. Allworthy.

MRS. MILLER: What is she doing here?

Mrs. Waters is ushered in by the maid.

PARTRIDGE: The very woman herself, sir.

Mrs. Waters looks straight at Allworthy.

MRS. WATERS: You probably don't recognize me.

ALLWORTHY: Indeed you are much changed, madam. But what business can you have with me?

MRS. WATERS: Such business as I can impart only to you, sir.

ALLWORTHY: Pray leave us.

Mrs. Miller, Partridge and the maid withdraw.

HALL OUTSIDE MRS. MILLER'S DRAWING ROOM.

Allworthy closes the door. Mrs. Miller and Partridge turn and kneel by it listening. They are seen in a succession of antic poses, as they react to what they but not we are hearing.

The door opens and Allworthy and Mrs. Waters march out. Mrs. Miller and Partridge scuttle aside. Camera tracks and pans with Allworthy and Mrs. Waters to reveal the rest of the hall shooting toward the door. At this precise moment Dowling the lawyer enters.

Zoom in to close-up of Dowling recognizing Mrs. Waters, starting in confusion.

Zoom in to close-up of Mrs. Waters recognizing Dowling.

MRS. WATERS: This sir, is the very man I was telling you about.

171

ALLWORTHY: But he is my steward.

MRS. WATERS: Nevertheless, this is the man.

Dowling is visibly more confused than ever.

ALLWORTHY: Do you know this lady?

DOWLING: That lady, sir.

ALLWORTHY: Look you, Mr. Dowling, if you value my favor do not hesitate but answer truly. Do you know this lady?

DOWLING: I have seen her, sir.

ALLWORTHY: Before my sister died, did she give you a letter for me, sir?

Dowling hesitates.

ALLWORTHY: Come with me, sir.

Firmly, Allworthy and Mrs. Waters march back into the drawing room followed by the apprehensive lawyer. Partridge and Mrs. Miller turn once more to the keyhole.

Allworthy opens the door, again startling the delighted eaves-droppers.

ALLWORTHY: Partridge, have my coach brought round at once.

As Partridge runs off, Blifil enters by the same door.

BLIFIL: Uncle, I have—

Allworthy taking in Blifil.

ALLWORTHY: Harkee, sir, before I return, you had better find the letter your mother gave to Dowling before she died.

Allworthy, Mrs. Waters, and Mrs. Miller march off leaving Blifil looking as if he were about to be hanged.

EXTERIOR. NEAR MRS. MILLER'S LODGINGS.

Partridge is ordering a carriage to convey the party to Newgate. Horses are quickly brought by two grooms, who begin to harness them. As the Allworthy group comes up Squire Western arrives too. He is in high old spirits, almost dancing along and singing, "Tol de rol de rol."

WESTERN: Good day neighbor. Are you going to see your bastard hang?

ALLWORTHY: On the contrary, Mr. Western. We are going to Newgate Jail to save him.

WESTERN: Save him? Save him? For what?

Sound is faded down on the dialogue. Mrs. Waters, who is in the foreground of shot, turns to camera and breaks the news why.

MRS. WATERS: And this is what Mr. Allworthy is saying to Mr. Western: My friend, Mr. Fitzpatrick, has now recovered and is no longer charging Tom with robbery. I couldn't be more pleased if he were me own son—which, it may surprise you to hear, he's not. For it was Mr. Allworthy's own sister Bridget who was Tom's mother, and I the one who put the baby in the Squire's bed. And that is what it says in the letter.

Fade up sound.

ALLWORTHY: So Tom is now my only heir.

Partridge and Mrs. Miller cheer.

WESTERN: Your heir? Did you say your heir?

The carriage is ready and Mrs. Waters, Allworthy and Mrs.

Miller get aboard.

ALLWORTHY: Yes, neighbor. To Newgate, Goody, and drive for dear life.

WESTERN: But I always loved that boy best. He shall have my Sophie by this hand.

But the coach has already rolled away, leaving Western frantically shouting after them. Partridge dourly checks his watch.

WESTERN: Tyburn, here I come! Come on, Miss Slouch!

ROAD TO TYBURN.

Panning over the heads of the spectators lining the route, the heads of the condemned men are visible, preceded by the shining helmets of the Horse Guards bearing javelins.

COMMENTATOR: And another old acquaintance has arrived, not only reinstated in the army but now in charge of the condemned. . . .

Northerton, gloating, is riding behind the cart. Camera tracks with the cart with the condemned men. They sing and whistle above the shouts of the crowd. Tom's expression is one of philosophical acceptance of his fate.

Tracking from their eyeline of a line of faces of all types looking upward at the (unseen) cart. Pertinent remarks are shouted by one or two of these spectators. One of them lifts a child to get a better view.

Tracking Tom's eyeline from the windows and balconies of the building spectators are waving and blowing kisses at the (unseen) cart.

Tracking with the condemned men. The change in their expression denotes that the excitement at the start of the journey has begun to wear thin. One of the condemned men wearily returns a kiss blown to him by one of the spectators.

NARROW LONDON STREET.

The Allworthy group ride up the street, at the end of which the backs of the crowd are seen beyond a barricade.

TYBURN.

The condemned men are being prepared by the hangman, who adjusts the ropes with the precision of an expert.

NEWGATE JAIL.

The Allworthy party storm through. Prisoners and visitors in the background react. A turnkey is present.

ALLWORTHY (*to Turnkey*): Turnkey, I have come to release a Mr. Tom Jones.

TURKNEY: We sent him off hours ago. He'll be strung up by now.

MRS. WATERS: But they can't hang him.

ALLWORTHY: But I have just procured this pardon for him.

MRS. WATERS: They can't hang an innocent man.

TURKNEY: They have done often enough before. (*He laughs.*)

ALLWORTHY: They won't have reached Tyburn yet. We must stop them. Come.

They turn and dash out. Turnkey turns away, laughing.

TYBURN.

Long shot of the whole scene. Tyburn was situated where Marble Arch is today. It was however then a vast open scape, stretching away into what is now Hyde Park. On the north side, all that could be seen were some ramshackle wooden stands, some built against a ruined brick wall. These stands are thronged with a mixture of all classes of the time, eager to see a cruel vicariousness with the spectacle. The ground is covered with a big crowd, with hucksters, thieves, fortunetellers, vendors of every tawdry kind. The gallows itself is a curious triangular improvised affair. Underneath the prisoners are roped on the cart and the cart driven away. Death is by strangulation except in a few fortunate cases, and the longer the suffering, the greater the entertainment. Soldiers, officials, crowd jostle each other so that it is difficult to tell where one begins and the other leaves off. There is a sequence of the preparations intercut sharply with the spectators' mounting anticipation.

Throughout the voice of the street singer:

STREET SINGER (*offscreen*):

    If he swing by the string.
    He will hear the bells ring,
    And then there's an end to Tommy.

178

He must hang by the noose,
And no hand'll cut loose,
The noose from the neck of poor Tommy.

ROAD TO TYBURN.

Allworthy party urge the carriage on at full speed.

ALLWORTHY: Faster! Faster!

TYBURN.

An official is holding the horses attached to the cart.

Panning with the hangman leaving the cart after finally checking the knot.

A line of soldiers roll their drums.

The black-hooded hangman signals.

Panning over the crowd roaring.

Close shot: Noose around Tom's head. He looks at the crowd.

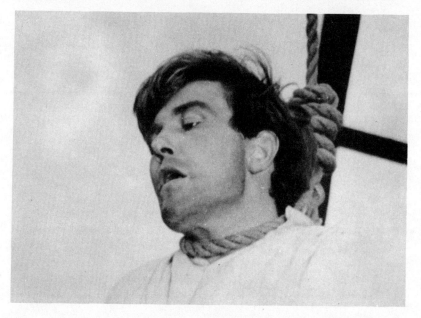

Northerton takes off his hat.

NORTHERTON: Better luck in the next world, Mr. Jones.

Close shot: Tom.

COMMENTATOR: To die for a cause is a common evil, to die for nonsense is the devil.

Northerton gives the signal.

The official lashes the horses and the cart lurches forward through the frame. Camera whip pans into a closish shot of Tom being jerked into the air. There is a great roar from the crowd. Zoom in to freeze on Tom's dangling legs.

COMMENTATOR: And it would be the devil's own nonsense to leave Tom Jones without a rescuer.

But after the first second's violence we realize that Tom is not dangling after all. Camera tilts up. Squire Western has ridden up and is supporting Tom astraddle on his shoulders. With his one free hand he slices the rope with his sword and they ride off.

NORTHERTON: Damn!

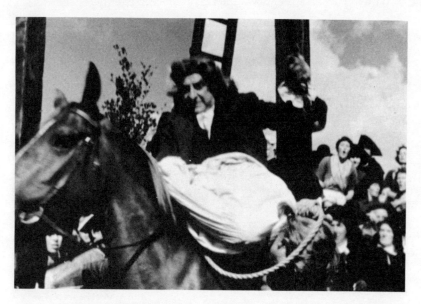

Western, with Tom at his back, gallops through the crowd, camera panning. The crowd goes mad with the bravado of his action and just as violently as they were against the prisoners before, they turn on officers, soldiers, hangman alike, and release the other prisoners.

Allworthy's coach rushes up, and he runs from it to meet Tom.
Close shot: Tom and Allworthy.

ALLWORTHY (*putting his arms around Tom*): Oh my dear boy, forgive me.

TOM: Forgive you?

ALLWORTHY: How can I ever make amends for those unkind, unjust suspicions I have held of you.

TOM: You have always used me kindly.

ALLWORTHY: No, nephew. I have used you cruelly.

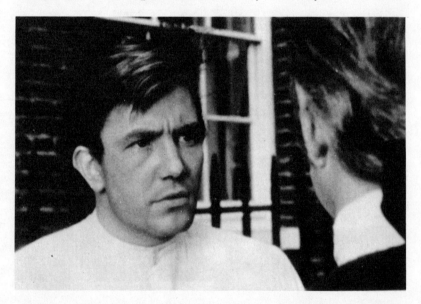

TOM: Nephew?

ALLWORTHY: Yes, you are indeed illegitimate. But your mother was not this lady but my sister Bridget.

TOM: Uncle!

ALLWORTHY: It is true, Tom.

Tom embraces Allworthy and they swing round.

WESTERN: Ah, this is no time for explanations, neighbor. Tom, thou art as hearty a cock as any in the kingdom. Go on after your mistress.

TOM: Alas, I fear I've sinned against her for all time. I doubt if she'll speak to me now.

MRS. MILLER: No, Tom. Don't say you've lost her yet. Go to her now.

MRS. WATERS: Go on, Tom.

MRS. MILLER: Go to her.

WESTERN: Go on, lad!

TOM: I will.

WESTERN: Go to her, lad! To her!

Tom goes to the front door, brushes back his hair and enters the building.

WESTERN'S DRAWING ROOM.

Tom crosses to Sophie and takes her hand before a long rectangular mirror. He then catches her in his arms and kisses her with an ardor he has never ventured before. At this instant, Western, who has been listening, bursts into the room with the rest of the company and, with his hunting voice, cries out:

WESTERN: Harkee, Allworthy, I'll bet thee a thousand pounds to a crown we have a boy tomorrow nine months.

Camera pulls back from close shot of Tom and Sophie kissing. This image is frozen.

COMMENTATOR: Happy the man and happy he alone,
   He who can call today his own,
   He who secure within can say:
   Tomorrow do thy worst! For I have lived today.

A Note on this Edition of
Tom Jones

The film script we publish here is considerably different from the text published by Faber and Faber, in London. In a letter granting us permission for this version, John Osborne remarked: "It depends what you want —what I wrote to go in on the floor or what came out as the completed film. It is obvious you want the latter and you may be right. Anyhow, go ahead as you wish." He noted that certain of the changes came from "actors who won't do what they're told and it doesn't matter much either way, though usually I prefer my own taste. Some [of the changes] were spontaneous, others accidents, in the way of film making. Some were editing, and again, some are improvements and others are not." In the case of slight variations in dialogue we have retained Mr. Osborne's phrasing.

Our main goals in preparing this edition were accuracy and readability. We strove to be faithful both to the script and to the film made from it. In the name of readability we began by eliminating such standard shooting script paraphernalia as, with each shot change, the endless repetition of the locale (for example, "Exterior" or "Interior" were dropped wherever irrelevant or redundant); place names of shooting sites ("Field behind Cerne Abbas"); time of day ("Day" after "Day" after "Day"; "Day for Night," where camera filters are indicated; etc.); also shot numbers (such data from the original as "380-382 Deleted" without further information can do little for the reader but arouse frustrating speculation).

The Faber text does not contain some ten scenes or parts of scenes to be found in the finished film, but it does include more than eighty shots cut from the picture. We decided to omit the latter; and we transcribed and inserted the former. Further, in many instances we added, deleted, or revised descriptions so as to correspond with what the spectator sees on the screen. Finally, and most important, we rearranged the sequence of scenes to proceed as they do in the film. Our decision to follow the movie's order was necessitated by our policy of illustrating the text. For scholars who wish to check ours against the Faber edition we print after this note, using the Faber numbers, a listing of our sequence. The word "new" there indicates almost every area where we added missing descriptions or dialogue— even though sometimes no more than a line or two; major additions are italicized (see page 192).

One typical if minor change: in the original the first two scenes between Tom and Molly were one sequence. Together they followed the Constable's encounter with Black George. In the film they are split, the first half occurring earlier, during Tom's first night prowling; the second half later, after the scene in which the Commentator identifies Thwackum, Square, and Blifil. Because of the discrepancy between the shooting script and the way Molly and Tom were directed and played, we removed from the second scene two of Mr. Osborne's lines: *"Tom looks at her dubiously for a moment, then shuts her mouth with a big final kiss"* and *"Molly flings her arms around Tom's neck."* To describe what in fact happens (see stills on pp. 22-25) we inserted in different places from the previous sentences: *"Molly fingers his nose and mouth"* and *"She gives him a big wet kiss and leans back."* Tom, it seems, was directed and played as a somewhat more passive creature than Mr. Osborne (and Mr. Fielding) wrote him. He doesn't initiate much; he "gets laid," as that telling Americanism has it, by Molly, Mrs. Waters, and Lady Bellaston. Our revised text and the stills occasionally reflect such distinctions as they show themselves in the action. Anyway, we assumed readers might be somewhat unsettled to read of Tom shutting her mouth with a kiss alongside frames showing him to be out of action, out of it, throughout.

Another, rather contrary example of revision occurs at the end of a farmyard scene between Squire Western and his sister (p. 77) where we added this: *"He claps one of the farm girls on the buttocks and falls into the hay on top of her";* also Western's words: "Oh, come on, my girl." Nearby in the text, Western's drunken fall from his horse (p. 76) is a further bit of business and commentary not in the Faber edition.

Film is a collaborative medium, a cooperative art. One would be tempted to put "of course" in that sentence, except that this truth receives constant challenge—if only implicitly, by omission—from the cult-of-personality critics.

Plainly the contribution to *Tom Jones* by producer-director Tony Richardson is an extraordinary one. We have had no chance to check with either Mr. Osborne or Mr. Richardson about the precise nature and extent of their collaboration here, but we can assume about the differences between script and film that almost every change was approved if not suggested by the writer. Mr. Richardson has directed most of Mr. Osborne's plays and movie scripts; their collaboration in art and business continues; they are partners in the company that produced *Tom Jones,* Woodfall Film Productions. Surely the contributions of cameraman Walter Lassally, editor Anthony Gibbs, and composer John Addison, not to mention the cast, are also most impressive and in some measure apparent to the non-professional. It is unfortunate that we have neither the space nor the exact information to describe in detail the making of this picture. Soon in this film book series, hopefully with as good a picture as this, we mean to include—in addition to stills and scenario, plus perhaps some of the variations of the latter—an informed account of "who did what and how" in the making of the movie. Something similar in certain ways to Lindsay Anderson's admirable study of Thorold Dickinson's *The Secret People,* the book called *Making a Film.*

Three sequences may suffice barely to suggest the style and inventiveness Mr. Richardson and his co-workers brought to the script. In each case we have left the text very much as in the Faber edition, adding only the dialogue to the first two sequences. These are the hunt (pp. 42-48), Tom's recovery (pp. 50-52), and Tom and Mrs. Waters eating (pp. 104-115). The text of each is a gem very much in the rough here, but each is testimony to Mr. Osborne's faith in the imaginations of his collaborators.

A contrasting method was used in dealing with the fight between Tom and Northerton (pp. 96-98). In the Faber edition, Mr. Osborne says of the fight only: *"Pan with Tom rushing at Northerton who escapes down the hill."* We have added some six sentences so as to give the barest outline of the action as Mr. Richardson devised it.

Perhaps a few more examples of what we added may explain if not justify what has been done. Many of the instances are relatively trivial: Mr. Osborne would have had Sophie on a white horse during the hunt; because she got a horse of another color, we dropped the adjective. Then, when Tom falls in with the Redcoats we felt obliged to insert the information that they go off across the countryside singing *Rule, Britannia*.

No mention is made in the Faber edition of the life-size male nude statue standing in Lady Bellaston's entrance hall; since Tom's reaction to it is a moment in the film, we added it. Conversely, for the rapid-fire silent comedy opening Mr. Osborne provided dialogue for most of the characters; since only the mouthing of what appears on the title cards is seen, we eliminated the extra lines.

Considerable passages of dialogue not to be found in the original have been inserted into the following scenes: that with Thwackum, Square, and Blifil, referred to above; the church scene; the burial of Mrs. Blifil; Tom's last go with Molly; Tom and the landlady at George Inn; Sophie and Honor with the same landlady; the first scene between Lord Fellamar and Sophie; the first between Allworthy and Mrs. Miller; also most of the scene between Partridge and Mrs. Waters, that between Allworthy and Partridge, and the last between Allworthy and Tom. Lastly, the street song is not referred to in the original.

Another typical change involves Mrs. Waters' Oedipus-Schmoedipus re-action to the news that Tom is her "son." Because the Faber text did not mention this moment (which produces one of the biggest laughs in the film), we have tried to describe it; further, one of the original scenes omitted concerns the same subject: Partridge, visiting Tom in jail, tells him that Mrs. Waters is Jenny Jones, his mother. Tom faints. Partridge, who has no idea of what happened in that hotel room in Upton, is astonished.

Some few times we have left in descriptions of action omitted from the completed film. The sounds of Tom and Molly rutting (p. 61) and of Squire Western's fart (p. 82) are not on the soundtrack. We include them for fun, not knowing whether taste, decorum, or the censor dictated their dele-tion from the film. Another case where we include action finally omitted comes at the beginning of the ball (pp. 135, 136). Mr. Osborne would have had this: "*Partridge grabs a likely girl and disappears. Tom questions every woman in sight. . . . Tom gets small change from many of the women. . . .*" A cross-cultural anthropological observation of some value may be found in the producers' mimeographed cutting continuity: there it is noted in capital letters that "THE SHOT OF MRS. WATERS EATING OYSTER . . . IS EXTENDED SEVEN FEET FOR AMERICAN VERSION." To see what we Ameri-cans presumably go for, that extra five odd seconds of swallowing banned for Britain if not everywhere else, see the upper two stills on page 113.

We would hope that Mr. Osborne will still feel at least as agreeably dis-posed to our edition as he was in his letter of June 22, 1964 in which he said, comparing a draft of ours with the Faber text, "Admittedly, yours is the more readable." We want to apologize to him now for any liberties he may find undue or uncivil, and also to thank him again for giving us his permission. We should also pay thanks here to Mr. David Picker of United Artists (financers and distributors of the film) for his many cour-tesies.

R. H.

1-18, *new,* 18-20b, 45, 20b, 26, 27, new, 28-30, new, 45, 46, 29, 30, *new,* 31-35, *new,* 37-39, 36, 40, new, 41-44a, 46a, new, 21, 22, 21-24, 25a, 46, 49, 47, 49, 50, new, 51, 50, 53, 54, 56, 57, new, 58, new, 59, 60, new, 61-64, new, 65, new, 66, 67, 69, 75-77, new, 78, 80, 81, 83-97, new, 98-104, 148, 105, 149, 150, 107, 108-113, *new,* 114-125, 131-142, new, 143, 144, 151, new, 152, new, 154, 155, 158, 157, new, 158, 159-161, new, 163, 164, new, 168, new, *new,* 169-172, 174, new, 175, new, 176, 177, 179, 181, new, 182, 187, 188, 183-185, 188-192, new, 194-196, 198-202, new, 203-206, *new,* 207, new, 208, 209, 211, 213, new, 230, 231, 214, 215, 232, 216-225, 201a, 233, new, 234, 241, 242, new, 243, new, 244, 245, new, 246-254, 236, 237, 235, 238-241, 259, new, 260, 256, 257, *new,* 267, 270, 271, new, 272-277, 261-264, new, 265, 278-287, new, 288-292, new, 293-295, *new,* 299, 296, 297, new, 298, new, 301, new, 300, 303-305, 307-312, 315-317c, new, 318, 320-323, 325, new, 326, 327, new, 328-336, 338, 340, 341, 344, new, 345, *new,* 346, 349, *new,* 350, 351, new, 352, new, 353-356, new, 357-360, 366, 377, new, 378, 379, 367-373, 383, 374, new, 375, 376, 385, 390, 391, new, 394, new, 396-401, new, 402, 403, new, 404, new, 405-410, 415, *new,* 408, 410, 411, new, 418, new, 419-423, new, 425-429, 432, *new,* 434, 435, 437, 438, 440, 441, 430, 431, new, 433, new, 442, 443, 439, 444-446, 448, 449, new, 450-452, 454, 455, new, *new,* 462, 465.